D0199953

# de-coding
# MARY
# MAGDALENE

# de-coding MARY MAGDALENE

## Truth, Legend, and Lies

### AMY WELBORN

Our Sunday Visitor Publishing Division
Our Sunday Visitor, Inc.
Huntington, Indiana 46750

The Scripture citations used in this work are taken from the *Catholic Edition of the Revised Standard Version of the Bible* (RSV), copyright © 1965 and 1966 by the Division of Christian Education of the National Council of the Churches of Christ in the United States of America. Used by permission. All rights reserved.

Every reasonable effort has been made to determine copyright holders of excerpted materials and to secure permissions as needed. If any copyrighted materials have been inadvertently used in this work without proper credit being given in one form or another, please notify Our Sunday Visitor in writing so that future printings of this work may be corrected accordingly.

Copyright © 2006 by Our Sunday Visitor Publishing Division, Our Sunday Visitor, Inc. Published 2006
11 10 09 08 07 06    1 2 3 4 5 6 7 8 9

All rights reserved. With the exception of short excerpts for critical reviews, no part of this work may be reproduced or transmitted in any form or by any means whatsoever without permission in writing from the publisher. Write:

Our Sunday Visitor Publishing Division
Our Sunday Visitor, Inc.
200 Noll Plaza
Huntington, IN 46750

ISBN-13: 978-1-59276-209-5
ISBN-10: 1-59276-209-3 (Inventory No. T260)
LCCN: 2006920100

Cover design by Monica Haneline
Cover art: The Granger Collection, New York; "The Magdalene," Bernardino Luini; oil on wood, c. 1525
Interior design by Sherri L. Hoffman

PRINTED IN THE UNITED STATES OF AMERICA

*Dic nobis, Maria,*
*quid vidisti in via?*
"VICTIMAE PASCHALI LAUDES," ELEVENTH CENTURY

# TABLE OF CONTENTS

# INTRODUCTION

*Equal-to-the-Apostles.*
*Blessed Sinner.*
*Spouse of Jesus.*
*. . . Goddess?*

The resume is impressive, if ultimately fanciful, but it actually only begins to touch on the many ways in which Mary Magdalene has been interpreted over the past two thousand years. Legends, myths, and wish fulfillment abound, but what's the truth — based on the evidence of history — about Mary Magdalene?

Mary Magdalene was an enormously important figure in early Christianity. She was, after the Blessed Virgin Mary, the most popular saint of the Middle Ages. Her *cultus* reveals much about medieval views of women, sexuality, sin, and repentance. Today, Mary Magdalene is experiencing a renaissance, not so much from within institutional Christianity, but among people, mostly women, some Christian, many not, who have adopted her as an inspiration and patron of their own spiritual fads, paths, and fantasies.

> **Mary Magdalene is the patron saint of contemplatives, converts, pharmacists, glove makers, hairdressers, penitent sinners, perfumers, sexual temptation, and women.**

This book is a very basic introduction to the facts and the fiction surrounding Mary Magdalene. We'll unpack what Scripture has to say about her identity and role in apostolic Christianity. We'll see how, very soon after that apostolic era, she was adopted by a movement that remade her image in support of its own theological agenda, a dynamic we see uncannily and, without irony, repeated today.

We'll look at the ways in which both Western and Eastern Christianity have described, honored, and been inspired by her, and how their stories about her have diverged. During the Middle Ages in the West, Mary Magdalene's story functioned most of all as a way to teach Christians about sin and forgiveness: how to be penitent, and with the hope of redemption open to all. She made frequent appearances in religious art, writing, and drama. She inspired many to help women and girls who had turned to prostitution or were simply destitute. She inspired Franciscans and Dominicans in their efforts to preach reform and repentance.

It all sounds very positive, and most of it, indeed, is. That's not, however, the idea we get from some contemporary commentators on Mary Magdalene's historical image.

Many of you might have had your interest in the Magdalene piqued by the novel *The Da Vinci Code*, by Dan Brown. In that novel, Brown, picking up on strains bubbling through pop culture and pseudo-historical writings of the past fifteen years or so, presents a completely different Mary Magdalene than the woman we meet in the Gospels and traditional Christian piety. She was, according to Brown, Jesus' real choice to lead his movement; a herald of Jesus' message of the unity of the masculine and feminine aspects of reality; a valiant and revered leader opposed by another faction of Jesus' apostles led by Peter; the mother of Jesus' child; and in the end, some sort of divine figure herself. Mary Magdalene is no less than the Holy Grail herself, bearing the "blood" of Jesus in the form of his child.

A glorious figure, indeed, was this Mary Magdalene, but one that a patriarchal church could not permit to flourish. So, the story goes, a new image of Mary was created: that of the penitent prostitute. This Mary Magdalene, degraded and demeaned, was the tool of a conspiracy to degrade and demean women in general, and to bury the "truth" of Mary Magdalene's leadership in early Christianity once and for all.

The theory fails on a couple of levels. First, there's no evidence to support it. That would seem like a fairly daunting obstacle.

There were certainly other interpretations of Jesus aside from the orthodox, apostolic experience and witness to him. We generally call these "heresies." Mary Magdalene was used, in minor ways, by some of these groups to embody their teachings, but — and this is the important point — *these groups' writings date from at least two centuries after the life of Jesus and have no connection to the events of that period.* The Mary-Peter competition is a myth and a misuse of these writings, which do have historical value — but for what they tell us about third- and fourth-century Gnosticism, not the Jesus movement of the first century.

**The heresy that some modern thinkers believe says the most about Mary Magdalene is Gnosticism. Gnosticism was a diffuse system of thought that taught, in general, that the material world was evil, and that salvation came from freeing the spirit imprisoned within the body. Christian Gnostics saw Jesus as a Gnostic teacher, and some Gnostic systems presented Mary as one of his wisest students.**

The image of Mary Magdalene as repentant sinner certainly is a medieval development, but as we shall see, it is the consequence, not of a political plot, but of a not-entirely illogical conflation of Mary with other figures in the Gospels.

The logic of the conspiracy theorists is flawed, too. If the patriarchy sought to demean the Magdalene, they did a terrible job of it, for it is difficult to see a figure who inspired prayer, devotion, countless good works, and who was honored and celebrated as a saint, and who was even popularly depicted in art as preaching, as a demeaned, degraded creature. Those who espouse these theories demonstrate, every time they write a sentence, an appalling, but not surprising, ignorance of historical and cultural context.

Brown's plot is a simplified version of some pretty complicated and esoteric theories about Mary Magdalene, a genre of spiritual speculation probably most strongly personified by Margaret Star-bird, author of *The Woman with the Alabaster Jar: Mary Magdalene and the Holy Grail* and *Mary Magdalene, Bride in Exile.*

Be assured that this kind of theorizing is not taken seriously by any scholars, no matter how secular or hostile to traditional Christianity those scholars might be. In my speaking on *The Da Vinci Code*, I often run into people who hold on to that novel, as well as its inspiration, *Holy Blood, Holy Grail*, *The Templar Revelation*, and Starbird's work, as serious exercises in history. They are not. A simple test to administer, if you doubt me, is as follows. Are these works used in courses on the History of Christianity at any university of any stripe, secular or religious? The answer: No.

In my research for this book, I have read much of the contemporary historical scholarship on Mary Magdalene. The only times the theories of Brown, Starbird, and their ilk are mentioned are in bemused footnotes on popular culture. The major work on the history of the Holy Grail written in the past few years, *The Holy Grail: Imagination and Belief*, published by Harvard University Press, does not mention Mary Magdalene in 370 pages of text.

Are they all part of the conspiracy, too?

The Magdalene-Spouse-Queen-Goddess-Holy-Grail theories are not serious history, so, frankly, we are not going to bother with them until the final chapter, and then only briefly. What we will be looking at — the history of the person and the imagery of Mary Magdalene — is daunting, rich, and fascinating enough.

The contemporary scholarship on Mary (and, indeed, on much of the history of Christian spirituality and religious practices) is growing so fast and is so rich that all I can do here is simply provide an introduction. A thorough, objective introduction, I hope, but the fact is that the burgeoning scholarship on Mary Magdalene is quite vast, and much of it, particularly that dealing with the medieval period, is not yet available in English. I have provided an annotated bibliography at the end of this book for those readers interested in pursuing this subject in more depth.

Our brief survey will undoubtedly be revealing, as we rediscover how deeply Mary Magdalene has been revered, used, and yes, misused and misunderstood by Christians over the centuries. The story, I hope, will be provocative in the best sense. For the fact is, the greatest interest in Mary Magdalene in the West today comes from those outside of or only nominally attached to the great course of traditional apostolic Christianity. Roman Catholics, in particular, seem to have lost interest in her, as, it must be admitted, they have in most saints.

Lots of people are listening to a Magdalene of their own making, a figure with only the most tentative connection to the St. Mary Magdalene of centuries of traditional Christian witness.

May the story recounted in the book play a part in reclaiming Mary Magdalene, so that we may hear her speak clearly again, as she does in the Gospels: for Jesus Christ, her Risen Lord.

**A NOTE ON TERMS**

- *Orthodox*, when capitalized, refers to the Eastern Orthodox Churches. When not capitalized, "orthodox" refers to Christianity that is self-consciously rooted in Scripture, apostolic teaching, and the tradition of the Early Church.

- *Cultus*, or "cult," when used in references to saints, does not have a derogatory connotation. It is a term used for the devotional practices that build up around a particular saint.

# One

# MARY OF MAGDALA

Before the legends, myths, and speculation, and even before the best-selling novels, there was something else: the Gospels.

The figure of Mary Magdalene has inspired a wealth of art, devotion, and charitable works throughout Christian history, but if we want to really understand her, we have to open the Gospels, because all we really know for sure is right there.

The evidence seems, at first glance, frustratingly slim: an introduction in Luke, and then Mary's presence at the cross and at the empty tomb mentioned in all four Gospels. Not much to go on, it seems.

But in the context, the situation isn't as bad as it appears. After all, no one besides Jesus is described in any detail in the Gospels, and even the portrait of Jesus, as evocative as it is, omits details that we moderns are programmed to think are important. Perhaps, given the context, the Gospels tell us more about Mary Magdalene than we think.

## Trustworthy?

Before we actually meet the Mary Magdalene of the Gospels, it might be a good idea to remind ourselves of exactly what the Gospels are and how to read them.

The word "Gospel" means, of course, "good news," or *evangel* in Greek, which is why we call the writers of the Gospels evangelists. The four Gospels in the New Testament have been accepted as the most authoritative and accurate writings on Jesus' life since the early second century. Even today, scholars who study early Christianity, whether they are believers or not, know that when studying Jesus and the early Christian movement, the Gospels and other New Testament writings are the place to begin.

Sometimes in my speaking on this issue, I have fielded questions about the reliability of the Gospels. A questioner will say something like, "Well, they were written *so long* after the events, how can we trust them to tell the truth?"

In addition, even those of us who have received some sort of religious education might have been taught, implicitly, to be skeptical of the Gospels. We're reminded, right off, that the Gospels are not history or biography, and that they tell us far more about the community that produced them than about Jesus himself.

In short, all of this gets distilled into the conviction that when it comes to early Christianity, all documents and texts are of equal value in telling us about Jesus. You can't pick the best according to historical reliability, so you pick the one with the "story" that means the most to you. So, if the Gospel of Mark displeases you, you can go ahead and create your Jesus from what you read in the *Gospel of Philip* or the *Pistis Sophia*.

Sorry, but it just doesn't work that way. As we will see in more detail when we get to the Gnostic writings, there is simply no comparison between the four canonical Gospels and other writings. The canonical Gospels were *not* written that distant from the events described — forty or fifty years — and were written in an oral culture that took great care to preserve what it heard with care; the community's history depended on it. When you actually read the Gospels, you see comments here and there from the evangelists themselves about what they were trying to do, and part of that involved, according to their own admission, being as accurate as possible (see Luke 1:1-4, for example).

No, the Gospels are not straight history or biography in the contemporary sense. They are testaments of faith. But they are testaments of faith rooted in *what really happened*. The evangelists, and by extension, the early Christians, were not about making up stories for which they would later, oddly, give their lives. They were not cleverly presenting their inner psychological transformations in the form of concrete stories. They were *witnesses* to the amazing action of God in history, through Jesus. They are testimonies of faith, yes, but faith rooted in the realities of God's movement in the world.

It's also good to listen to Gospel critics carefully. More often than not, those who disdain the Gospels are quick to claim some other text as "gospel," as the source of truth. Their choice of what to believe usually has far less to do with historical reliability than it does with other factors.

So, no, not all historical texts are equally reliable. When it comes to Jesus and the events of the mid-first century, the canonical Gospels are really the only place to begin.

Now, on to Mary Magdalene.

## Magdala

Luke introduces us to Mary Magdalene in chapter 8 of his Gospel:

> "Soon afterward he went on through cities and villages, preaching and bringing the good news of the kingdom of God. And the twelve were with him, and also some women who had been healed of evil spirits and infirmities: Mary, called Magdalene, from whom seven demons had gone out, and Joanna, the wife of Chuza, Herod's steward, and Susanna, and many others, who provided for them out of their means." (Luke 8:1-3)

So here she is: a woman from whom Jesus had driven seven demons, joined with other women, also healed by Jesus, who had left their lives behind to follow him.

Mary is mentioned first in this list, as she is in every list of female disciples, in every Gospel, similar to the way that in lists of the twelve apostles Peter's name always comes first. The precise reason for Mary's consistent preeminence is impossible to determine, but we can guess that it might have much to do with her important role related to the Resurrection, as well as to recognition of her faithfulness to Jesus.

These women "provided for them out of their means." This might mean one of two things, or both: that the women assisted Jesus and his disciples by preparing meals and so on, or that they supported them financially. The second explanation is supported by the presence of Joanna, the wife of a member of Herod's court, on the list. Perhaps some of these women were, indeed, wealthy enough to give Jesus' ministry a financial base. (Some legends about Mary have played off of this, as we will see later, suggesting that she was quite wealthy and actually owned the town of Magdala.)

What stands out about Mary is that she's identified, not by her relationship to a man, as most women would be at that time, but to a town. This indicates that Mary wasn't married, and perhaps even that she had outlived her father and other male relatives: she was a single woman, able to give support to Jesus out of gratitude for what he had done for her.

Magdala was located on the western shore of the Sea of Galilee, about four miles north of the major city of Tiberias. Today, it is a village with a few hundred inhabitants, some abandoned archaeological digs, and only the most inconspicuous memorials to its most well-known inhabitant.

"Magdala" is derived from the Hebrew *Migdal*, which means "fortress" or "tower." It was also called "Tarichea," which means "salted fish," a name which reveals the town's primary industry during the first century, the salting and pickling of fish. Excavations led by Franciscans in the 1970s revealed a structure that some think was a synagogue (others a springhouse), as well as a couple of large villas and, from later centuries, what might be a Byzantine monastery. Magdala is described by Josephus, a first-century Jewish historian, as having forty thousand inhabitants, six thousand of whom were killed in one of the battles during the Jewish

Revolt (A.D. 66-70), but most modern historians believe those numbers are far too high.

Jewish tradition suggests that Magdala was ultimately destroyed as a punishment for prostitution, and another strain holds that in ancient times Job's daughters died there. Pilgrim accounts from the ninth through the thirteenth centuries report the existence of a church in Magdala, supposedly built in the fourth century by St. Helena, who discovered the True Cross in Jerusalem. By the seventeenth century, pilgrims reported nothing but ruins at Magdala.

### Possessed

Mary — like Peter, Andrew, and the other apostles — walked away from life as she knew it, abandoned everything to follow Jesus. Why?

*". . . from whom seven demons had gone out."*

Exorcism is an aspect of Jesus' ministry that many of us either forget about or ignore, but the Gospels make clear how important it is: Mark, in fact, describes an exorcism as Jesus' first mighty deed, in the midst of his preaching (1:25). Some modern commentators might declare that what the ancients referred to as possession was nothing more than mental illness, but there is really no reason to assume that is true. The "demons," or unclean or evil spirits, we see mentioned sixty-three times in the Gospels were understood as forces that indeed possessed people, inhabiting them, bringing on what we would describe as mental problems, emotional disturbances, and even physical illness. The symptoms, however, were, to the ancient mind, only that: symptoms. The deeper problem was the alienation from the rest of the human family and from God produced by this mysterious force of evil.

In the world in which Jesus lived, seven was a number that symbolized completion, from the seven days of creation (Genesis 1:1-2:3) to the seven seals on God's book in Revelation (5:1) and the seven horns and eyes of the Lamb in the same vision (5:6). Mary's possession by seven demons (also explicitly mentioned in Mark 16:9) indicates to us that her possession was serious and overwhelming — total, in fact. She was wholly in the grip of these evil spirits, and Jesus freed her — totally.

So of course, she left everything and followed him.

It's worth noting now, even though we'll discuss it more later, that nowhere in the New Testament is the condition of possession synonymous with sinfulness. The "sinners" in the Gospels — the tax collectors, those who cannot or will not observe the Law, the prostitutes — are clearly distinguished from those possessed. Some Christian thinkers have linked Mary Magdalene to various sinful, unnamed women in the Gospels because of her identification as formerly possessed. There may be reasons, indeed, to link Mary to these women, but possession is not one of them, because the conditions — possession and sinfulness — are not the same thing in the minds of the evangelists.

## Disciple

The evangelists used the texts, memories, and oral traditions they had at hand to communicate the Good News about Jesus. Because they were human beings, their writing and editing bears the stamp of their unique concerns and interests. Just as you and a spouse might tell the same story, emphasizing different aspects of it to make different points — perhaps you want to tell the story of your missed flight as a warning about being organized and prepared, and he wants to tell it as a way to highlight the need to go with the flow — the evangelists shaped the fundamental story of Jesus in accord with what struck them as the most significant points of his life and ministry, what their audiences most needed to hear.

In the eighth chapter of his Gospel, Luke has finished introducing Jesus, and is ready to really help his audience understand what being a disciple means. He begins by describing who is following Jesus — the Twelve and the women — and then offers a general description of what Jesus' ministry is about. Jesus then tells his first parable (the parable of the sower and the seeds, which is the first parable Jesus relates in all of the Gospels), then quickly calms a storm, performs another dramatic exorcism, raises a little girl back to life, and in the midst of it tells his followers, firmly, that his blood relations are not his family, but rather those who "hear the word of God and do it" (Luke 8:21).

So that's the context of the introduction of Mary Magdalene and the other women — not just to set the stage, to complete the cast of characters, because Luke, like all of the other evangelists, didn't have vellum to spare to do such a thing. Every word he wrote had a purpose, and it was very focused — here, to set before us, in quick, strong strokes, what this kingdom of God was all about. What do we learn from the presence of the women?

First, we learn that women are present, period. Women were not chattel slaves in first-century Judaism, by any means, but neither were they often, if ever, seen leaving their ordinary lives to follow a rabbi. In fact, scholar Ben Witherington describes this conduct as "scandalous" in the cultural context (*Women in the Ministry of Jesus* [Cambridge University Press, 1984]):

> **"We know women were allowed to hear the word of God in the synagogue but they were never disciples of a rabbi unless their husband or master was a rabbi willing to teach them. Though a woman might be taught certain negative precepts of the Law out of necessity, this did not mean they would be taught rabbinic explanations of Torah. For a Jewish woman to leave home and travel with a rabbi was not only unheard of, it was scandalous. Even more scandalous was the fact that women, both respectable and not, were among Jesus' traveling companions."**
> (Witherington, p. 117)

And not just any women, either. As we noted earlier, Mary Magdalene was once possessed by seven demons. In this culture, those possessed were ostracized — one man Jesus exorcised is described as living in a cemetery (Luke 8:27). Mary Magdalene, formerly at the margins of society, has been transformed by Jesus and is now welcomed as a disciple. The barriers of class, too, are broken, Luke hints, with the presence of Joanna, the wife of a person of stature. In God's kingdom, Luke makes clear, the world we know is being turned upside down.

Just as every phrase and scene in the Gospels is carefully chosen under the inspiration of the Holy Spirit, so are the parts of the Gospel related. We meet Mary Magdalene here, but we will not see her again for many chapters — until the Passion narrative begins. But when we do encounter her — again, with the other women — here's what she will be doing: she will be standing near the cross, she will then be preparing Jesus' body for burial, and later she will see and witness to the empty tomb, and encounter the risen Jesus.

Mary will be serving, still. She serves, watches, and waits, the only remaining link between Jesus' Galilean ministry, his Passion, and the Resurrection. She is introduced as a grateful, faithful disciple, and that she will remain, a witness to the life Jesus brings. Already, there's a sort of mystery: what were these demons? What exactly happened to Mary? The evangelists don't tell us, perhaps because they and Mary herself knew that life with Jesus is not about looking back into the past, but rather rejoicing in God's power to transform our lives in the present.

### Questions for Reflection

1. What do we know about Mary Magdalene's life from the Gospels?
2. What does her presence in Jesus' ministry tell you about the kingdom of God that Jesus preached?
3. How has God acted in your life with power? How do you respond to that? How would you like to respond?

## Two

# 'WHY ARE YOU WEEPING?'

Luke is the only evangelist to mention Mary Magdalene before the Passion narratives, but once those events are set in motion, Mary is a constant presence in all of the Gospels, without exception. For the first few centuries of Christian life, it is her role in these narratives that inspired the most interest and produced the earliest ways of describing Mary Magdalene: "Myrrh-bearer" and "Equal-to-the-Apostles."

### At the Cross

In both Matthew (27:55) and Mark (15:40-41), Mary Magdalene is named, first in the list of women watching Jesus' execution. Luke doesn't name the women at the cross, but he does identify them as those who had "followed him from Galilee." John also mentions her presence (19:25), but his account highlights the presence of Mary, the mother of Jesus, and Jesus' words commending her to John's care.

After Jesus' body is taken down from the cross, Mary and the other women are still there. Matthew (27:61) and Mark (15:47) both specifically mention her as seeing where Jesus' body was laid, and Luke again refers to the "women ... from Galilee" (23:55), whose identity we are expected to understand from Luke's early mention of their names in chapter 8.

> "Love is as strong as death. This was seen in the Lord's passion, when Mary's love did not die." (*The Life of St. Mary Magdalene and of Her Sister St. Martha*, by Rabanus Maurus (translated and annotated by David Mycoff) [Cistercian Publications, 1989], p. 61)

Finally, as the Sabbath passes and the first day of the week dawns, the women still remain, and the Twelve are still nowhere in sight. Matthew describes Mary Magdalene and "the other Mary" (not the mother of Jesus, but probably the Mary, mother of James and Joseph, that he had mentioned in 27:56) coming to "see" the tomb. Mark and Luke get more specific, saying that the women have come to anoint Jesus' body. John, interestingly enough, in chapter 20, ignores any other women, and focuses on Mary Magdalene. She comes to see the tomb, finds the stone moved and the tomb empty, and runs to tell Peter.

At least one early critic of Christianity seized on Mary Magdalene's witness as discrediting. As quoted by the Christian writer Origen, the second-century philosopher Celsus called her a "half-frantic woman" (*Contra Celsus,* Book II: 59), thereby calling into doubt the truth of her testimony of the empty tomb.

What is striking about John's account is that even though Peter and others do indeed run to the tomb at Mary's news and see it empty, that is all they see. They return, and after they have gone away, Mary remains, alone at the tomb, weeping. It is at this point that, finally, the risen Jesus appears.

Of course, Jesus appears to Mary and other women in the Synoptic Gospels as well. In Matthew (chapter 28), an angel first gives them the news that Jesus has risen from the dead. The women then depart to tell the Twelve, and on the way they meet Jesus, they worship him, and he instructs them to tell the disciples to meet him in Galilee.

In Mark (chapter 16), they meet the angel first as well, and receive the same message as Matthew describes, and are, unlike the joy described by Matthew, "afraid." (Fear and lack of understanding on the part of disciples is a strong theme in Mark's Gospel, by the way.)

Mark presents us with a bit of a problem, because the oldest full manuscripts of Mark, dating from the fourth century, end at 16:8, with the women afraid, and with no appearance of the risen Jesus described. Manuscripts of a century later do contain the rest of the Gospel as we know it, continuing the story, emphasizing Jesus' appearance to Mary Magdalene, and identifying her as the one from whom he had exorcised seven demons. She sees him, she reports to the others, and they don't believe it. Jesus then appears to "two of them" (perhaps an allusion to the encounter on the road to Emmaus we read about in Luke 24) who then, again, report the news to the Twelve who, again, do not believe it. Finally, Jesus appears to the disciples when they are at table, and as is normal in the Gospel of Mark, their faithlessness is remarked upon.

> Some modern scholars suggest that Mark 16:8 is the "real" ending of this Gospel, which would mean that it contains no Resurrection account. Others, including the Anglican Bishop N. T. Wright, a preeminent scholar of the New Testament, argue that when one looks at Mark as a whole, it is obviously building up to the Resurrection, including prophecies from Jesus himself. Wright theorizes that the original ending was perhaps lost (the ends of scrolls were particularly susceptible to damage), and that what we have now is an attempt by a later editor to patch up that lost ending, but not in a way inconsistent with Mark's intentions.

The theme of disbelief also runs through Luke. Interestingly enough, this Gospel doesn't recount an encounter between the women (who are finally again specifically identified) and Jesus, but only the appearance of "two men" in "dazzling apparel," who remind them of Jesus' prophecies of his death and resurrection. The women, no longer afraid, go to the apostles, who, of course, dismiss their tale as idle chatter.

What's clear in these Synoptic Gospels is, first, the strong sense of historical truth about the accounts. Rationalist skeptics would like to dismiss the Resurrection as a fabrication, but if it is, then the storytellers did a terrible job, didn't they?

After all, if you were creating a myth that would be the origins of your new religion, would you write something in which the central characters — the first leaders of this same religion — were so filled with fear and doubt that they appeared weak?

If you were making up the story of the Resurrection from scratch, you would, as a person living in the first century, in the Roman Empire, and presumably as a Jew, only be able to think about this resurrection business in the terms and concepts available to you. And, as N. T. Wright has so ably demonstrated in *The Resurrection of the Son of God* (Augsburg Fortress Publishers, 2003), even the first-century Jewish world, which did believe in a resurrection of the body, saw it in completely different terms — that it would eventually happen to everyone, at once, at the end of time (Wright, pp. 200-206).

And in general, when you read over the Resurrection accounts in the Gospels, you are immersed in an account in which people are afraid, confused, in awe, and eventually profoundly overjoyed. There is a veil drawn over the core event — the Resurrection itself is never described because, of course, none of the witnesses saw it. They saw the empty tomb, and they saw the risen Jesus. A clever fabricator and mythmaker would not have woven his account with such nuance, and would probably have offered a direct account of the event itself, perhaps even with a clear explanation of what it all meant. But that's not what we read, and somehow, ironically, all of the confusion and human frailty is powerful evidence for the truth of the account.

Most importantly for us, a first-century mythmaker would not have featured women as the initial witnesses of these formative events. It is inaccurate to say that first-century Jews did not accept women as reliable witnesses at all. There was, of course, no unified system of law within Judaism, and what was practiced was dependent upon which rabbi's interpretation of the Law was used. Some rabbis did, indeed, hold the opinion that women were not reliable witnesses, but others disagreed and counted a woman's witness equal to a man's.

However, the fact that a woman's reliability as a witness was disputed, unclear, and not consistently accepted, would, it seems, discourage a fabricator from using women as his source of information that the tomb was indeed empty. It certainly wouldn't be the first choice to come to mind if your aim was to present a story that was easily credible, would it?

> "[And] so that the apostles [the women] did not doubt the angels, Christ himself appeared to them, so that the women are Christ's apostles and compensate through their obedience for the sin of the first Eve.... Eve has become apostle.... So that the women did not appear liars but bringers of truth, Christ appeared to the [male] apostles and said to them: It is truly I who appeared to these women and who desired to send them to you as apostles." (Hippolytus, third century, quoted in *Mary Magdalene: Myth and Metaphor*, by Susan Haskins [Berkley, 1997], pp. 62-63)

### 'Noli Me Tangere'

John's account of Jesus' post-Resurrection appearance to Mary, chapter 20, adds more detail than the Synoptics. She comes to the tomb while it is still dark — recall how John's Gospel begins, with the wonderful hymn describing the Word bringing light into the darkness — and she sees that it is empty, and then runs to get the disciples. Peter and another disciple come to the tomb, see it for themselves, but leave, since, as John says, they didn't yet understand "the scripture" — perhaps the Hebrew Scriptures as they would be later understood by Christians.

Mary stays, though, weeping (John 20:11). She peers into the tomb (the level of detail in this account is fascinating) and sees two "angels in white" who ask her why she is crying. She says, sadly, "They have taken away my Lord, and I do not know where they have laid him" (John 20:13). She then turns and sees another figure; we are told it's Jesus, but she doesn't know until he speaks her name (John 20:16)

One of the more well-known moments in this account comes in John 20:17, when Jesus says to Mary, in the famous Latin rendering of the words, "*Noli me tangere*," which has commonly been translated, "Do not touch me." This, however, is not the most accurate translation — either in Latin or English — of the Greek, which really means something like, "Do not cling to me" or "Do not retain me."

So, no, Jesus is not engaging in misogynistic behavior here. Nor is he (as some modern commentators suggest) alluding to a supposed former intimate relationship between him and Mary. This is not about touching; it is about understanding who Jesus is and what his mission is. After all, Thomas is invited to touch the wounds of Jesus in John 20:27. No, Jesus tells Mary to let go of him, to look beyond the moment, to the future. After all, his very next words direct her to go to the apostles and tell them, "I am ascending to my Father and your Father, to my God and your God" (John 20:17). Knowing Jesus for who he is, we cannot stand still. We have to move, get out, and share the marvelous news that in Jesus the barriers between humanity and God are dissolved.

Which, of course, Mary Magdalene does. All of the evangelists agree that she was the first to announce this Good News to the apostles, who, more often than not, responded with skepticism. But such is the way it has always been. God always chooses the least in the world's eyes, the unexpected and the despised, to do his most important work. To see this event only through the prism of politics, and to be inspired by it to think only about gender roles and such, is to be willfully blinded to the greater reality: Jesus lives, Jesus saves, and as we are touched by this truth, we are, at the same time, called to go out and share it.

> **"Be the first apostles to the apostles. So that Peter . . . learns that I can choose even women as apostles."** (Gregory of Antioch, sixth century, quoted in Haskins, p. 89)

### Mary of the Bible

Mary Magdalene's future in Christian spirituality and iconography is rich, evocative, and even confusing, as we'll see in subsequent chapters. But it all begins here, with powerful simplicity and themes that will resonate through the centuries.

Mary Magdalene, healed of possession, responds to Jesus with a life of faithful discipleship. As spiritual writers and theologians will point out, she's like the Bride in the Song of Songs. She's like the Church itself, called by Christ out of bondage to the evils that pervade our world, giving ourselves over to him in gratitude, waiting with hope by the tomb, even when all seems lost, and rewarded, in a small, grace-filled moment, when, in the midst of darkness, we hear him call our name.

### Questions for Reflection

1. What does Mary's desire to hold on to Jesus symbolize to you? How do you experience this in your own life?
2. Why is Mary referred to as "Apostle to the Apostles"?
3. What can Mary's fidelity teach you about your own relationship to Jesus?

# Three

# THE REAL MARY?

O ver the past twenty years, interest in Mary Magdalene has exploded. Books, websites, seminars, and celebrations of her feast day on July 22 have multiplied, as many in the West, particularly women, look to her for inspiration.

Ironically, though, much of this interest in this great Christian saint is being fueled by texts other than the Christian Scriptures. The popular websites devoted to Mary Magdalene refer to her as "The Woman Who Knew All" (www.magdalene.org). One of the more popular treatments of Mary Magdalene, *The Woman with the Alabaster Jar: Mary Magdalene and the Holy Grail*, by Margaret Starbird, emphasizes Mary as "Bride and Beloved" of Jesus.

And, of course, there's *The Da Vinci Code*, the mega-selling novel that has brought these depictions of Mary Magdalene to a mass audience. Brown's novel brings it all together in one convenient package: Mary Magdalene was the spouse of Jesus, bore his child, and was the person he really wanted to lead his movement. This movement, of course, was about nothing the New Testament suggests it is, but was rather a wisdom movement dedicated to help humanity reunite the masculine and feminine principles of reality.

So in this context, Mary Magdalene was the "real" Holy Grail, since she was the vessel that carried Jesus' child and his teaching. But she's more: she's a "goddess" — a mythical figure through whom the divine can be encountered.

It's all very confusing. It's also ironic, given the constant modern criticism that the claims of traditional Christianity are suspect because they can't be "proven," or because the texts upon which its claims are based are too ancient to be trusted. The modern devotion that so many seem to have to this figure of Mary is actually based, in part, on far less trustworthy sources and has no relation to the Mary we meet in Scripture.

So where does it start? Of course, much of this revisioning is rooted completely in the present, in a mishmash of conspiracy theories, false history, and wishful thinking that we will address in the last chapter. But the truth is that Mary Magdalene wouldn't be the subject of interest from many of her contemporary fans outside traditional Christianity if it weren't for some other ancient texts: the writings produced by Gnostic Christian heresies.

## Secret Knowledge

Here's the short version. From about the second through the fifth centuries, a movement that we now call "Gnosticism" was popular in many areas around the Mediterranean basin. "Gnosticism" is a word derived from the Greek word *gnosis*, which means "knowledge." Although there were various Gnostic teachers and movements over the centuries, most of them shared a few common characteristics, succinctly described by Father Richard Hogan in his book *Dissent from the Creed: Heresies Past and Present* (Our Sunday Visitor, 2001):

> **"Gnostics claimed a special knowledge, a gnosis. Included in this special gnosis was an understanding that there was God Who created the spiritual world and a lesser anti-god who was responsible for the material (evil) world. Gnosticism represents a belief in dualism. There is a good and an evil. Evil is material and physical. Good is spiritual and divine.**
>
> **"According to the Gnostics, a disaster at the beginning of the world had imprisoned a divine 'spark' in human beings, i.e., in the evil world of material Creation. This divine element had lost the memory of heaven, its true home. Salvation consisted in knowing that this 'spark' existed and liberating it from the human body."** (Hogan, p. 43)

The creation myths of Gnosticism that describe this imprison-
ment are quite complex and intricate. Just as intricate were the Gnostic visions of what salvation was about. The emphasis, naturally, was
on knowledge, rather than faith, life, or love. The way to salvation
involved knowing the truth about human origins and then knowing the way to progress, both in this life and the next, through the
various layers of reality that were imprisoning that sacred spark.

Early Gnosticism, which predates Christianity, drew from many
sources, including Platonic philosophy and Egyptian mythology.
Christian Gnosticism used the Gospels and other Christian traditions, eliminating elements that were not consistent with Gnostic
thinking. So, for example, Gnostic Christian teachers taught that
Jesus was not really human — since the material world is evil.
Valentinus, who lived around the year 150 in Rome, taught an
extraordinarily complex story of Jesus being the product of the
yearnings of Sophia — the personification of wisdom. Historian
David Christie-Murray describes it in the following way:

> "Christ, who brings the revelation of gnosis (self-consciousness),
> clothed himself with Jesus at baptism and saves all spiritual
> mankind through his resurrection, but had only a spiritual body.
> Men can now become aware of their spiritual selves through
> him and return to their heavenly origin. When every spiritual
> being has received gnosis and becomes aware of the divinity
> within himself, the world-process will end. Christ and Sophia,
> after waiting at the entrance of the Pleroma [the center of spir-
> itual, divine life] for spiritual Man, will enter the bridal chamber
> to achieve their union, followed by the Gnostics and their higher
> selves, their guardian angels." (A History of Heresy [Oxford University
> Press, 1989], p. 29)

This is just one example, but Gnostic Christianity is really simply a variation on this theme: Creation is evil. Jesus was not fully

human. He did not suffer or die. Redemption cannot, of course, be achieved through such a means, for it involves the material body, which is sinful anyway. Salvation is not available to all, but only those with special knowledge. This way of thinking infiltrated many other systems of the time, including Christianity.

Those who tried to merge Gnostic thinking with Christianity produced writings, some of which survive, mostly in the context of quotations in the works of Christian writers arguing against them. In the late nineteenth century, some Gnostic Christian texts, not seen before, were discovered, and even more in the mid-twentieth century. The discovery of these texts caused a stir among some who believed that, more than giving an insight into a Christian heresy, these texts opened a world to what they believed could be the real story of Christianity that was concealed by orthodox Christian leaders.

Consequently, over the past century or so, these Gnostic texts have been rediscovered and reinterpreted. Some have taken their existence as proof that there was a whole other, and long-hidden, response to Jesus' ministry, one with roots as ancient as those we see in the Gospels, and just as legitimate. The modern re-visioning of Mary Magdalene as Jesus' bride, as the special recipient of his wisdom, and as the foundress of an alternative mode of Christianity owes much to the fascination with these Gnostic writings.

Unfortunately — or fortunately, depending on your point of view — what we actually know of the history of early Christianity just can't back up these exalted claims for Mary Magdalene or even of any substantive link between Jesus' ministry and Gnostic Christianity and Gnostic writings.

The simplest way to put it is this: Gnostic Christian texts tell us a lot about Gnostic Christian heresies in the second through the fifth centuries. They tell us nothing about the historical figures of Jesus, Mary Magdalene, Peter, or the origins of Christianity in the first century.

So what follows is that these Gnostic texts tell us nothing substantive about the real Mary Magdalene, either, and that all those who use them in that way are engaging in, at best, misguided efforts, and, at worst, deceitful misuses of historical materials.

But it continues, nonetheless, and for a reason: this technique of suggesting that the Gnostic Christian texts reveal secret truths about early Christianity and who Jesus "really" was and what he "really" taught serves to undercut not only the New Testament but also the Church that produced it and is formed by it.

As I've done talk radio shows discussing this matter, I've heard it again and again: "All of these works were written so long after the events they describe — they're all equally dependable and undependable. What version of Jesus you choose doesn't matter, for there's no way to know the truth, anyway."

That's just not true. Early Christianity was an enormously complex movement, about which we cannot claim to know everything. But we do know — and any serious scholar will affirm — that Jesus did not teach Gnostic platitudes and did not marry Mary Magdalene, who then embarked on a life of teaching Gnostic platitudes of her own and emanating divine energy.

It just didn't happen.

But because these Gnostic texts are so important in so many contemporary treatments of Mary Magdalene, we definitely need to look at them and understand what they're really about.

## Know Nothing

It's somewhat challenging to describe Gnosticism because it wasn't an organized movement, a religion, or even a homogeneous philosophical school. Perhaps the best way to describe it would be to compare it to the self-help movement of our day. For some reason, in the last part of the twentieth century, this notion of the importance of self-esteem took hold in our culture and infiltrated almost every aspect of life, including religion. Two hundred years ago, Christian thinkers and preachers of any denomination would have been appalled at the suggestion that a goal of Christian faith is to help the believer feel better about herself or help her overcome insecurities and self-doubts. On the contrary, despite their differences, Christians and Protestants alike would have described the goal of the Christian life as believing rightly and shaping your life in a way that meet's God's standards and spares one an eternity in hell.

Gnosticism was, of course, more complex and cosmic than this. But it's a decent example to start with, for, like the self-esteem movement, Gnosticism wasn't confined to groups that identified themselves explicitly as "Gnostic" and separate from other religions. It infiltrated and impacted almost everything it rubbed against, including Judaism and Christianity.

You can see the problems. Gnosticism wasn't a minor movement. In most major cities of the Roman Empire during these centuries, Gnosticism and even Gnostic Christianity thrived. Most of our knowledge of Gnostic Christianity comes from its Christian opponents, great theologians like St. Irenaeus, Tertullian, and St. Clement of Alexandria, who all wrote against Valentinus, for example, and quoted copiously from his writings in doing so.

But independent copies of some Gnostic Christian texts do exist, and it's these texts that form the basis of the modern, non-Christian devotion to Mary Magdalene.

## Ancient Words

In the nineteenth century, several discoveries broadened scholarly comprehension, and eventually popular understanding, of Gnosticism. An ancient work of the Christian Hippolytus, *Refutation of All Heresies*, lost for centuries, was discovered in 1842 in a Greek monastery. This work, of course, quoted many heretics, including Gnostics. More important to many was the rediscovery (in the British Museum) and then translation of *Pistis Sophia* (into English in 1896), a probably third-century work in which Mary Magdalene — and Mary, the mother of Jesus, by the way — figure prominently in dialogue with Christ. Snippets of other Gnostic texts existed, but the real revolution in this area came in 1945 with the discovery in Egypt of the Nag Hammadi library, a collection of Coptic texts, bound in leather, and dating from the late fourth and early fifth centuries, that included many Gnostic works (as well as a partial copy of Plato's *Republic*). Hidden in jars and stored in caves, it is thought that the library belonged to a Gnostic Christian monastery.

The Nag Hammadi collection contains fifty texts in thirteen codices (a form of book), three of which — the *Gospel of Philip*, the *Gospel of Thomas,* and the *Dialogue of the Savior* — are of interest to those intrigued with Mary Magdalene. Other Gnostic texts believed to mention Mary Magdalene, and found outside the Nag Hammadi library, are the *Gospel of Mary* and the *Pistis Sophia*. These texts emerged from different periods and reflect different strands of Gnosticism. All are discussions between Jesus and various other figures, mostly about the nature of the soul, the afterlife, and the end of time. Let's take a brief look at how each of them treats the figure called "Mary."

### *Pistis Sophia* (third century)

This work consists of extensive dialogues between Jesus, who has been on earth teaching for eleven years since the Crucifixion, and others, including women. Mary, his mother, takes an enormous role, and several times a "Mary," not explicitly identified as either his mother or anyone else, including Mary of Magdala, is mentioned and praised for her understanding, and is even the subject of envy by other disciples.

### *The Gospel of Philip* (third century)

This work is made up of dialogues and sayings of Jesus in conversation with his disciples. It mentions the Magdalene, "who was called his companion," along with "Mary his mother and her sister," as three who "always walked with the Lord." The passage, quite provocative to some, ends with the sentence, "His sister and his mother and his companion were each a Mary."

This work also contains the passage describing Jesus as kissing Mary Magdalene often and the rest of the disciples disapproving, asking, "Why do you love her more than all of us?" Jesus' answer is obscure, but implies that she is more enlightened than they are. Those who see this kiss bestowed by Jesus as an expression of a unique companionate relationship are missing the point in a big way. In Gnosticism, the kiss is symbolic. As one scholar points out: "The Logos lives in those whom he has kissed, hence the disciples' jealousy, for they are not yet worthy of the kiss" (Jorunn Jacobsen Buckley, quoted in *The Making of the Magdalen: Preaching and Popular Devotion in the Later Middle Ages*, by Katherine Ludwig Jansen [Princeton University Press, 2000], p. 27).

### *The Gospel of Thomas* (third century)

This, the most well-known of all the Gnostic writings, is a collection of sayings, many of which are also found in the canonical Gospels, but with a heavy dose of the androgynous themes that contemporary readers find so appealing. A "Mary" is mentioned once (the other female character is a "Salome"), as Peter asks Jesus to make her leave. Jesus, in a passage that is not often quoted by modern fans of this gospel, says, "I myself will lead her in order to make her male, so that she too may become a living spirit resembling you males. For every woman who will make herself male will enter the kingdom of heaven."

### *The Gospel of Mary* (third century)

This is another dialogue, this time beginning with Jesus but ending with a "Mary," who is identified as the one Jesus loved "more than the rest of the women" and as the primary teacher, in a rather subtle competition, it seems, with Peter.

## A 'Few' Problems

These, then, are the basic texts that modern devotees of Mary Magdalene use to support their case that she was an important leader of early Christianity, and probably in an intimate relationship with Jesus — but even if not, that her wisdom was esteemed by him above the other male disciples, and that there was friction between Mary Magdalene and the male disciples. This friction, in the eyes of some, reflects a real, historical division in early Christianity between those who followed Mary as a teacher and those who followed Peter.

There are numerous problems with using these documents to support this view of Mary Magdalene. Let's look at a few of them.

To begin with, this position assumes that the Gnostic texts reflect first-century events. The simple truth is, they do not. No scholars date any of the texts earlier than the second or third centuries. The view they present of Jesus, his teachings, and his ministry are radically different from what we read in the Gospels, which were all composed before the end of the first century. Scholars of all types consistently consider the Gospels and the rest of the New Testament to be the starting point for studying the history of early Christianity. They may disagree on what the texts mean, but none would suggest, for example, that the *Gospel of Mary* is of equal value with the canonical Gospels in determining what the early Jesus movement was all about.

No, the Gnostic texts "tell" us exactly what they should: namely, the ways that Gnostic Christian heretics took the basics of the Christian story and molded them to fit Gnostic thinking. Since some elements of Gnosticism were interested in questions of gender and androgyny, that concern is reflected in some texts, and in the roles played by female figures. They might reflect a greater role for women in some Gnostic sects, or they might even reflect a desire to demean the role of Peter, recognized as the chosen leader of orthodox Christianity.

But if you take the time to read these works yourself, you'll see that they are radically different from the canonical Gospels in tone and content. (The Gnostic texts are not long, and all are available on the Internet. The *Gospel of Mary*, at least the fragment that we have today, is reproduced in full in Appendix B of this book.) The canonical Gospels, with all of their very human, flawed figures, are reflective of an attempt to present events accurately, through the prism of faith, certainly, but accurately nonetheless. The Gnostic writings are preachy, tendentious, obtuse, and ... well ... Gnostic in their concerns.

So the contemporary thinkers who suggest that a strand of "Magdalene Christianity" was born from Mary's early leadership that was eventually suppressed by those loyal to Peter are basing their conclusions on the most tenuous of threads: that these Gnostic writings, written some two hundred years after the fact by Gnostics, reflect an ancient, hidden relationship between Mary and Jesus.

Let's take this one step further. Who's to say that the "Mary" mentioned in all of these writings is, each and every time, Mary Magdalene?

After all, there are only a couple of incidents — in the *Gospel of Philip* and *Pistis Sophia* — in which the Magdalene is specifically mentioned. The much-vaunted *Gospel of Mary* speaks only of a "Mary," does not specify the Magdalene, and gives no identifying clues to tie her into the historical figure of Mary Magdalene, despite modern editions tacking "Magdalene" on to the title. Even the *Gospel of Philip*, which has been held up by many as evidence of a "companion" relationship between Mary Magdalene and Jesus, is not as clear as it seems on who that Mary is. A close reading of the text indicates, a growing number of modern scholars suggest, that the female figure is a composite, mythical "Mary," representing the feminine aspect of reality.

One of the features of some contemporary celebrations of Mary Magdalene is that the Gnostic writings indicate a tension between her and Peter and the other disciples, thereby implying a separate strand of "Magdalene Christianity." Entire books have been written on this. That view, of course, is dependent on reading these Gnostic texts as if the Mary in conflict with the disciples is, in fact, Mary Magdalene. That's by no means certain.

In the *Pistis Sophia*, Mary, the mother of Jesus, is described as being in conflict with the disciples. On a couple of other occasions, another Mary is described in the same way, and many assume this Mary is Mary Magdalene, although she is not explicitly identified in this way. However, some scholars — looking at the way this Mary is described, as "blessed among women" and "called blessed by all generations" — believe that a case could be made for identifying this Mary as Jesus' mother. At the very least, it is not certain at all that she is Mary Magdalene, who does, in turn, play a prominent role in the dialogues in Book Two of the work.

Scholar Stephen J. Shoemaker summarizes this perspective:

> In summary then, the Gnostic Mary's identity is by no means a simple matter, nor is her identification with Mary of Magdala as certain as it is frequently asserted in modern scholarship. The particular spelling of the name Mary is in no way a reliable criterion distinguishing the two women, even though this is the most frequently advanced argument in favor of the Gnostic Mary's identity with Mary of Magdala. If anything, the spellings Mariam and Mariamme appear to favor an identification with Mary of Nazareth, as I have demonstrated elsewhere. Likewise, the writings of the New Testament fail to resolve this problem, since they show both Marys to have equally been important figures in early Christian memory. Even the Magdalene's role as *apostola apostolorum* in the fourth gospel does not tip the balance in her favor, since in early Christian Syria, where it seems most likely that the Gnostic Mary traditions first developed, it was believed that Christ first appeared to his mother, Mary of Nazareth, commissioning her with a revelation to deliver to his followers.
>
> Moreover, despite frequent assertions to the contrary, there is significant evidence that early Christians occasionally imagined Mary of Nazareth in situations similar to those in which the Gnostic Mary is found: she converses with her

risen son, expounds on the cosmic mysteries, and reveals her son's secret teachings to the apostles, with whom she is occasionally seen to be in strife. Such is especially evident in the *Pistis Sophia*, a text whose interpretation has been tightly controlled by the last century's interpretive dogmas. Both this text and the Gospel according to Philip make clear that the Gnostic Mary traditions do not have only a single Mary in view. Although many will no doubt continue to take refuge in the Gospel according to Philip's description of Mary Magdalene as the Savior's favorite, we should not forget that the New Testament identifies Mary of Nazareth as the 'favored one,' who has 'found favor with God.' ("Rethinking the 'Gnostic Mary': Mary of Nazareth and Mary of Magdala in Early Christian Tradition," *Journal of Early Christian Studies*, 9:4, pp. 588-589)

Why take so much time to unpack this? Because it's terrifically important in getting Mary Magdalene right. Many contemporary activists have adopted Mary Magdalene as a representative of an alternative vision of Christianity, based partly on wishful thinking, partly on her role in the canonical Gospels, but confirmed, in their minds, by the evidence of these Gnostic writings. In them, they see traces of an ancient tension, an ancient movement within the followers of Jesus that held up Mary Magdalene as a wisdom teacher, as the one Jesus designated as his successor.

Their vision sounds plausible to those unfamiliar with the original texts, or even to those who only read them in translation, interpreting them according to the assumptions of the promoters of "Magdalene Christianity." But ancient texts are usually not as simple to interpret as we think or would like to think.

A careful, objective reading shows, quite simply, first, that the figure of Mary of Nazareth played an unquestionably important role in some Gnostic texts. Why hasn't she been chosen and celebrated by modern interpreters as the special chosen one of Jesus? Second, while Mary Magdalene does appear in these texts, most of the evidence for "Magdalene Christianity" is derived from the presence of a "Mary" who is, in fact, not clearly identified as Mary Magdalene, and is probably either a mythical composite female figure or Mary of Nazareth. Most importantly, though, all of the figures in these Gnostic writings really function on a level of symbol more than historical reality. Scripture scholar John P. Meir sums up the case quite well:

> "I do not think that the . . . Nag Hammadi codices (in particular the *Gospel of Thomas*) offer us reliable new information or authentic sayings that are independent of the NT [New Testament]. What we see in these later documents is rather the reaction to or reworking of NT writings by . . . gnostic Christians developing a mystic speculative system." (*A Marginal Jew: Rethinking the Historical Jesus*, Vol. I [Doubleday, 1991], p. 140)

As we will see throughout the rest of this book, Mary Magdalene is a great saint, and a woman worthy of our interest and honor. But there is simply no evidence that she was who her modern interpreters would like her to be. The Gnostic texts that they use to make the case tell us nothing about early Christianity in the first century, and the "hints" that some read in them, suggesting an ancient tradition being preserved about a leadership role for Mary Magdalene in competition with Peter, are by no means certainly about Mary Magdalene, and in some cases might even refer to Mary, the mother of Jesus.

Further, if you read the documents yourself, you will see how ambiguous they really are, how easily they lend themselves to selective reading, and even how, in parts, the Gnostic writings contradict what their modern proponents would have them say.

In short, when dealing with Mary Magdalene, Jesus, and the Gnostics, don't trust the interpreters. Go right to the source.

### Questions for Reflection

1. What was Gnosticism? Do you see traces of Gnostic thinking in the world today?
2. How do some try to use Gnostic writings in regard to Mary Magdalene? What are the flaws to their approach?
3. What do the Gnostic writings tell us about the Mary Magdalene of history?

# Four

# APOSTLE TO THE APOSTLES

While Gnostic writers were — or perhaps weren't — writing about Mary Magdalene, favored student of the Gnostic Jesus, orthodox Christian writers had a few things to say as well during those early centuries of Christianity.

She didn't dominate the scene, but a few thinkers found her an intriguing figure, helpful in understanding the nature of faith and redemption. She's represented in art from the period as well, most often in her role as "myrrhophore" — one of the women bringing oils and spice to Jesus' tomb.

It's that theme that we see most frequently: Mary Magdalene as faithful disciple and witness to the empty tomb, and then, digging a little deeper, Mary as the New Eve and Mary as the Church, symbolized with power and passion in the Old Testament Song of Songs.

Those who think that the Gnostics were more appreciative of Mary Magdalene than were orthodox Christians who were perhaps busy demonizing her might be in for a surprise. Many early Church Fathers had no problem identifying Mary Magdalene in quite exalted terms: "Apostle to the Apostles" and "Equal-to-the-Apostles," titles which may be now neglected in the West, but which remain her primary identification in Eastern Christianity to this day.

## 'Come, My Beloved'

It might be helpful, before getting to Mary herself, to set the scene. When we talk about the "early Church" and the "early Church Fathers" and their writings, what exactly do we mean?

For the purposes of this chapter, "early Church" means Christianity up to the late sixth century, at which point we start creeping into the early Middle Ages, or the Dark Ages, as they are quite unfairly called.

During this period, Christianity spread throughout the Middle East, into Africa, far into Europe, and even into India. The time began, of course, with most of that area (with the exception of India) as part of the Roman Empire, where Christianity was illegal. By the time the sixth century rolled around, the old Roman Empire had collapsed, new kingdoms and empires had taken shape, and Christianity was not only legal in all of them, but was the established religion in most as well, a situation that would last until the rise of Islam in the eighth century.

By the end of the first century, a basic church structure of presbyters (priests) and bishops was beginning to evolve (we can even see this in the New Testament: for example, in the First Letter of Paul to Timothy). The religious landscape was not the same as it is today: there were no seminaries, no universities, and of course, no publishing houses or religious newspapers. But there were theologians, spiritual writers, and bishops, who wrote and preached. Many of their works have survived and are available in English — even on the Internet — today.

Most commonly, the texts that we can read that give us an idea of what these Christians were thinking and how they believed and practiced their faith are:

- Defenses of Christianity against skeptics and heretics.
- Commentaries on Scripture.
- Homilies.
- Letters.
- Catechetical instructions.

And not coming from individuals but from church communities were liturgies and, beginning in the fourth century, decrees from gatherings of bishops.

So you see, although there is much we don't know, a great deal of evidence has survived that gives us an excellent picture of Christian life in its first five centuries of life. It is not as mysterious and ambiguous as some claim. Christian thinkers were seeking to deepen their understanding of the Gospel, in the context of a culture that was extremely hostile to them, as well as intellectually and religiously diverse.

There's a good reason people still read the writings of these early Church Fathers. Their situation was not that different from ours. They were dealing honestly and tenaciously with the most fundamental aspects of Christian faith, and they were trying to make them understandable to a world that, while skeptical, was obviously deeply in need of Christ. Two thousand years is a long time — but not long enough for human nature and humanity's need for Christ to change.

These early Christian writers viewed the literal truth of Scripture — in which they firmly believed, by the way — as a starting point. From that factual level, they routinely set off exploring nuance, making connections, and discovering useful analogies and allegories. Patristic writing is extremely rich in that way.

So for them, Mary Magdalene was more than a woman at a tomb, just as Jesus had been more than a man on a cross. In Jesus, all of history is redeemed and all of creation is reconciled to God. Into this richness step ordinary men and women like you and me, people like Peter, Levi, John, and Mary. As they live and move in Jesus' shadow, listening and responding to him, they, too, become more. Their actions evoke other figures' responses to God's outstretched hand. Their doubt, faith, sin, and redemption become more than just their own, as we look at them and see echoes of our own lives and, in fact, of the whole human story.

So, for example, when some of these writers meditated on Mary Magdalene, they saw her responding to the Good News of redemption and eternal life — in a garden. It recalled another scene, at the beginning of salvation history, also in a garden in which a woman and a man disobeyed God, and humanity fell. And so, for some, Mary Magdalene became a sort of New Eve, long before the title had attached itself to the Virgin Mary. For example, St. Cyril of Alexandria, who lived in the fifth century, said that because of Mary Magdalene's witness at the empty tomb, all women were forgiven of Eve's sin (Haskins, p. 89). St. Augustine, St. Gregory the Great, St. Ambrose, and St. Gregory of Nyssa also made the connection:

> "She is the first witness of the resurrection, that she might set straight again by her faith in the resurrection, what was turned over by her transgression." (St. Gregory of Nyssa, *Against Eunomius* 3.10.16, quoted in *The Resurrection of Mary Magdalene: Legends, Apocrypha, and the Christian Testament*, by Jane Schaberg [Continuum International Publishing Group, 2002], p. 87).

The image of a woman grieving and waiting in a garden evoked another image for Christians: that of the great love poem in the Hebrew Scriptures, the Song of Songs (also known as the Canticle of Canticles or Song of Solomon). The third-century Christian writer Hippolytus made a great deal of this in his own commentary on the Old Testament book. He brings in not only Mary Magdalene but also the other women reported at the tomb in the various Gospels, and sometimes in confusing ways. The female image, rooted in specific figures, becomes more generally symbolic but, with Mary Magdalene as one of them, echoes the deep desire of the bride in the Old Testament book, her desire for her beloved, as they seek Jesus at the tomb:

> " 'By night, I sought him whom my soul loveth': See how this is fulfilled in Martha and Mary. In their figure, zealous Synagogue sought the dead Christat.... For she teaches us and tells us:

By night I sought him whom my soul loveth." (Hippolytus, third century, quoted in Haskins, p. 61)

Finally, writers during this period cited Mary Magdalene for her witness at the tomb and sharing the Good News with the apostles. Hippolytus, who was also a bishop, referred to her as "Apostle to the Apostles." Other Church Fathers also praised Mary for her role as a witness, some holding that through her example, all women are honored and, in a sense, redeemed.

A fourth-century Eastern poet named Ephrem used this image, although, confusingly to us, he conflates Mary Magdalene and Mary, the mother of Jesus, in the following (as we saw in the last chapter, this was a characteristic of Syrian Christianity in this period):

"At the beginning of his coming to earth
A virgin was first to receive him,
And at his raising up from the grave
To a woman he showed his resurrection.
In his beginning and in his fulfillment
The name of his mother cries out and is present.
Mary received him by conception
And saw an angel at his grave."

(Quoted in Haskins, p. 90)

In this early period of Christian reflection, theological and spiritual writers worked in a relatively simple garden. Scripture — both Hebrew and Christian Testaments — was their primary source. Their sense of who Mary Magdalene was and of her importance for Christians was derived completely from that. She was historically significant because she was the first to see the empty tomb and the Risen Christ. Her role evoked other women in other gardens, and another layer of reflection was woven, celebrating Mary Magdalene as a New Eve or as representing the Church as the expectant bride seeking her bridegroom, Christ — but all because of what the Christian tradition had testified about her role in the events of the Resurrection.

The story of Mary Magdalene obviously does not end here, for at this point — the fifth and early sixth centuries — some images, quite familiar to us today, have not yet appeared. What of the penitent Magdalene? The prostitute? The evangelizer of the French? Where these came from we shall soon see, as we enter the Middle Ages, a period of intense creativity and legend-building, in which the evidence of Scripture was revered, but popularly viewed as only the beginning to far more interesting tales.

### Questions for Reflection

1. Why did early Christian thinkers refer to Mary Magdalene as the "New Eve?"
2. Why did they connect Mary Magdalene to the Song of Songs?
3. What do you think of this approach to interpreting Scripture? Do you find it helpful or not?

# Five

# WHICH MARY?

"Myrrh-bearer," "New Eve," "Apostle to the Apostles." To early Christian thinkers, Mary Magdalene served as a symbol of humanity yearning for new life and love in God, and she represented that very redemption, discovered at the empty tomb in the garden, as Eve had represented our fall in another garden.

The vision is all very scriptural, all very tied to Mary's role in the Resurrection appearances and her fidelity to Jesus through his arrest and crucifixion.

Throughout the period, however, there were hints: hints of confusion, hints of an even broader and deeper well from which to draw as Christians contemplated the meaning of this woman in the life of Jesus and the Church. Remember the mind-set, so different from our own.

We're obsessed with history and facts, a clear division between past and present. Christians of this period thought and prayed much more cosmically. The world was heavy with meaning — every bit of it. God's ways, so vast and so deep, could be glimpsed in the richness of revelation, in the events of the past, and in the people who had, in awe and bliss, walked with and listened to the Lord. Contemplating a figure like Mary Magdalene was a process in which the past was interpreted in light of the even more distant past, in the reality of the present and hope for the future. Ever determined to be faithful to the truth, it was still imaginative, far-reaching, and provocative in the best sense: provoking the listener, the reader, and the pray-er to look deeper, to look further, to see the connections, great and small, that bind us to one another and to God.

So, as Christianity grew and evolved, so did its thinking, drawing from the deep well of Scripture and Tradition, confronting questions, trying to give answers to puzzling silences. What does it mean, exactly, to say that Jesus is fully divine and fully human? What does our redemption mean? How are we saved from sin?

And in the midst of all of this fascinating theological and spiritual conversation, a smaller question, perhaps, but one that was to have great implications: There are so many Marys and unnamed women in the Gospels. Are they different people? Could they be one and the same? Is there more to Mary Magdalene than we thought?

## Full of Marys

The confusion about Mary Magdalene is rooted in two factors:

- There is more than one "Mary" identified in the Gospels, even aside from Mary, the mother of Jesus. Crucial here is Mary of Bethany, who is the sister of Martha and Lazarus, mentioned several times in the Gospels (Luke 10:38-42; John 11:1-44; John 12:1-11).
- There are also unnamed women who seem to share characteristics with Mary Magdalene. Most importantly, immediately before Luke introduces Mary Magdalene in chapter 8, he tells the story of a nameless repentant woman who anoints Jesus (Luke 7:36-50).

The way that these two points have worked themselves into the confusion is . . . confusing. But in essence, it comes down to this: Mary of Bethany is described as anointing Jesus in John 12:1-11. Some came to associate this story with the story of the anointing in Luke 7, as well as other stories of women anointing Jesus' feet in other Gospels. Add to this that Mary Magdalene is described as coming to Jesus' tomb to anoint him. This aura of grieving and anointing, as well as a sharing of names, led some to think that all of these women might be the same: Mary Magdalene.

Finally, another element in the mix is that of sin and repentance. As we noted before, Mary Magdalene is explicitly described, both by Luke and John, as being a woman from whom Jesus drove out seven demons. This is not a state identical with being a "sinner." However, later commentators, perhaps not understanding this, did, indeed, confuse the concepts, giving more strength to the association between the anointing penitent woman in Luke 7, and even the woman caught in adultery in John 8:1-11.

Even in those first centuries, when the spotlight was on Mary Magdalene as "Myrrh-bearer" and "Apostle to the Apostles," some thinkers were puzzled. Tertullian, writing in the second century on the scene between Mary and Jesus in the garden after the Resurrection, referred to her as "the woman who was a sinner."

The great preacher and bishop of Milan, St. Ambrose, wondered about the identities of the various Marys. There is even a Syrian tradition (noted in Chapter 3 of this book on the Gnostic interpretations of Mary) that replaces Mary Magdalene, in scenes with the risen Jesus, with Mary, his mother.

St. Augustine, writing in the late fourth and early fifth centuries, did not confuse Mary Magdalene with any other figure, but did suggest that the woman who anoints Jesus in Luke 7 could be Mary of Bethany, sister of Martha and Lazarus. Augustine praised Mary Magdalene and, consistent with the thinkers who preceded him, highlighted her role as a first witness to the Risen Christ:

> **"Then, as John informs us, came Mary Magdalene, who unquestionably was surpassingly more ardent in her love than these other women who had ministered to the Lord; so that it was not unreasonable in John to make mention of her alone, leaving those others unnamed, who, however, were along with her, as we gather from the reports given by others of the evangelists."** (St. Augustine, *Harmony of the Gospels*, Book III: 24:69)

The ambiguity of some of the Gospel accounts, as well as natural human curiosity, led some to question, and others to make some connections between these various women in the Gospels. However, at the end of the sixth century, the die was cast for centuries to come by Pope St. Gregory I.

## Three in One

Gregory I is one of two popes to be formally called "the Great," the other being St. Leo I (who reigned from 440-461 and, among other things, convinced Attila the Hun to not invade Rome). His greatness stems from his keen and energetic response to the times in which he lived — a period of disaster, flux, and disintegration — in which he knew only Christ could provide sure, steady hope.

Gregory was pope during a time in which the land we now know as Italy was under constant siege from various barbarian Germanic tribes, primarily the Lombards and the Franks. In addition, natural disaster in the form of a flood devastated Rome in the beginning of his papacy. He met the challenges, drawing from his Benedictine monastic background, with its strong sense of order and service to the poor.

Gregory was also very present to the people of Rome, going out to various churches on Sunday, preaching sermons that were suffused with scriptural references, many of which have survived — along with hundreds of his letters — today.

One of his most well-known homilies was preached, it is believed, on September 21, 591, in the Basilica of San Clemente in Rome. The subject of the homily, referred to as Homily 33, was the story of the repentant woman, from Luke 7. Here, Gregory makes the leap and identifies this woman with Mary Magdalene:

> **"She whom Luke calls the sinful woman, whom John calls Mary, we believe to be the Mary from whom seven devils were ejected according to Mark. And what did these seven devils signify, if not the vices? . . . It is clear, brothers, that the woman previously used the unguent to perfume her flesh in forbidden acts. What she**

therefore displayed more scandalously, she was now offering to God in a more praiseworthy manner. She had coveted with earthly eyes, but now through penitence these are consumed with tears. She displayed her hair to set off her face, but now her hair dries her tears. She had spoken proud things with her mouth, but in kissing the Lord's feet, she now planted her mouth on the Redeemer's feet. For every delight, therefore, she had had in herself, she now immolated herself. She turned the mass of her crimes to virtues, in order to serve God entirely, in penance, for as much as she had wrongly held God in contempt." (Quoted in Haskins, p. 93)

In this homily, Gregory is not just examining Mary Magdalene for her own sake. He's offering her up to his listeners as an example of the possibility of repentance and the promise of forgiveness. That's sometimes forgotten in contemporary discussions of the imagery here, which tend to excoriate Gregory for not just an apparent error in interpretation, but also misogyny and a desire to demean Mary Magdalene. It's clear that no such diminishment was in his mind.

Modern readers tend to forget an important point about Christian life in past centuries. Today, many of us operate out of a conviction, not of original sin, but original blessedness. We have a vision of human life that has inched from a realistic, yet hopeful view of humanity and its weakness to a deep conviction that everyone is okay, all the time, no matter what — that we're all "good" and in no need of redemption. This, it should be obvious, was not the ancient way of looking at things.

Gregory was talking to a congregation that was certainly not frantically convinced of its damnation, but which was at the same time quite realistic about sin. His listeners understood the power of temptation in their lives and their need for God. They mourned their sinful pasts and sought Christ's mercy and strength to go and sin no more.

So, here, Mary Magdalene isn't being held up as a figure to be scorned. The impact of Gregory's associating her with Luke's sinful woman was not to degrade her, nor was it intended to do so. She was held up as a model: a different sort of model than the "Apostle to the Apostles" imagery, certainly, but still a model and an inspiration. This was no plot to demean women. It was an expression of a desire to find our own story of loss and hope in the Gospel story.

The historical study of religious expression is very complex and challenging, as historians try to trace the origins and development of concepts, ideas, and practices. This moment in the year 591 gives us an unusual insight that we don't normally have with other saints' cults. Right here, we can see, quite clearly, the origins of an entirely new development in hagiography. As historian Katherine Ludwig Jansen notes, "By appropriating the identity of Luke's sinner, Gregory the Great's Magdalen inherited a sinful past; by assuming the character of Mary of Bethany, the Magdalen acquired siblings (Martha and Lazarus) and became associated with the contemplative life. It was an audacious but not capricious piece of exegesis. Gregory was evidently responding to questions about Magdalenian identity, which, as we have seen, was already the subject of not a little confusion" (Jansen, p. 33).

Gregory preached yet another homily on Mary Magdalene, one in which he expanded on her life as a contemplative, implicitly appealing to the Martha and Mary story in Luke 10. This image, too, would remain a part of the Magdalene legend and take hold later in the Middle Ages.

**The only major dissent from the conflation of the Marys came in 1519 with the publication of a tract by Jacques Lefevre d'Etaples, who appealed not only to Scripture but also to the**

writings of St. Jerome and St. Ambrose, to support his view of the separate identities of the Marys. Others, including St. John Fisher (who was eventually executed in anti-Catholic England), argued for the tradition of the unity of identity. Lefevre was accused of heresy, fled France, but eventually returned as tutor to the king's children. The unified theory of the Marys held, and was accepted by the reformers Luther, Zwingli, and Calvin as well (Haskins, p. 246).

How, we might wonder, could two homilies from a single pope, no matter how "great," have such an impact on hundreds of years of subsequent Christian devotion? Well, there may not have been quick communication in those days, but there *was* communication. Notable homilies of notable preachers — especially popes esteemed for their preaching — were collected, copied, disseminated, and read by other thinkers and preachers. Not long after Gregory's reign, the practice of writing down saints' lives, mostly as aids for preaching, became a common practice. Mary Magdalene is no minor figure in the Gospels, and the appeal of her story was great, especially as themes of penitence began to dominate Christian spirituality in the early Middle Ages. What Gregory began, other preachers and hagiographers picked up, elaborated on, and disseminated in turn. By 720, we find a feast of Mary Magdalene noted on a martyrology compiled by the Venerable Bede, a church historian from Britain. The date is July 22, the same date we celebrate today.

And so it begins — the next, very complicated stage in the life of Mary Magdalene in the Church. Devotion to the Blessed Virgin Mary was at its infancy at this point, and existent mostly in the Syrian and Egyptian churches. What we'll see as the Middle Ages progress, though, is that while devotion to the Blessed Virgin will flourish, so will devotion to Mary Magdalene, but for different reasons, and out of a different set of needs and motivations, the groundwork for which was laid in the perhaps providential "mistake" of Gregory the Great.

### Questions for Reflection

1. What were the various Gospel stories that Gregory used to talk about Mary Magdalene?
2. In what ways might we say that the content and purpose of what Gregory did is actually consistent with what the Scriptures tell us about Mary Magdalene?
3. What do you think is the difference between what Gregory did and what the Gnostics did with the figure of Mary Magdalene?

# Six

# 'THE GOLDEN LEGEND'

When we think of the Middle Ages, it's tempting to think of the period as a mere blip in time, in which knights, serfs, monks, and wenches traded in simplistic faith and ignorance, waiting for the light of the Renaissance and the Enlightenment.

Wrong. Ignorant people, as a rule, do not build cathedrals.

It was no blip in time, either. The medieval period of European history was almost *one thousand* years long, usually dated from the final fall of Rome in the late fifth century to the early fifteenth century. That's quite a long time, plenty of time for the development of layered, complex religious traditions and spiritual movements.

The story told about Mary Magdalene during those centuries reflects that richness. It is, of course, inaccurate to speak of a single "story," for there were many. Legends about her life during the ministry of Jesus and after the Resurrection flourished. Different shrines claimed her relics. Miracles were claimed and recorded in books, and she was a terrifically popular figure in art, music, and drama — more hymns were written featuring Mary Magdalene than any other saint. And how did they speak of her? What did these legends say?

The tales went down many paths, but tended to focus on three areas:

- Mary's sinful past and conversion.
- Her devotion to Jesus during his life.
- Her evangelizing work in southern France.

When medieval people thought of Mary Magdalene, they never forgot her presence at the tomb and her role as the "Apostle to the Apostles" — she was still celebrated for that. But other images came to dominate during the period: tears, anointing, preaching, contemplation, and devotion. They saw her, pre-conversion, as a symbol of Vanity and Luxury. They marveled at images of her floating in contemplation, fed by angels.

## All in the Family

By the early medieval period, Pope St. Gregory the Great's identification of Mary Magdalene with Mary, the sister of Martha, and then with the penitent woman in Luke 7 had taken firm hold in the West, as his sermons were circulated and studied. Remember that the Eastern Church never made this association, continued to see all three of these women as distinct figures, and celebrated Mary Magdalene primarily for her role as "Myrrh-bearer" and "Apostle to the Apostles."

But in the West, the connection was firm and almost unassailable. Gregory's homily moved thinking in that direction, and a few centuries later, stories and legends based on his interpretation had begun to evolve. In one part of Europe, her story had been conflated with that of the hermit Mary of Egypt and was circulated, by the middle of the ninth century, as her *vita eremitical.*

Around the same time, another set of stories circulated that originated in Cluny, a great French Cistercian monastery, traditionally attributed to a monk named Odo. These, called the *vita evangelica*, brought together and embellished all of the Gospel stories about Mary Magdalene, which by this time, of course, would include stories that, in the Gospels, were about Mary, the sister of Martha and Lazarus, and Luke's penitent sinner.

In the eleventh century, the final piece of the puzzle emerged: the *vita activa,* or stories which claimed that Mary Magdalene had spent most of her life after the Ascension in southern France, which she evangelized, and where she was buried.

From this point on, most lives of Mary Magdalene included all three of these elements: the Gospel stories, the preaching in France, and the contemplative life.

Saints' lives were a very important part of medieval Christian devotion. They were used by priests in their homilies, and were told and retold as a way for ordinary people to see how God had been at work in the world — and still was. There are many saints' lives from the medieval period still in existence, but perhaps the most convenient place to get a sense of how medieval people heard the Mary Magdalene story is through a collection called *The Golden Legend*.

*The Golden Legend*, or *Legenda Aurea*, was so called because of its enduring popularity. It was compiled, probably about 1260, by Jacobus de Voragine, a Dominican who eventually became archbishop of Genoa and was beatified by Pope Pius VII in 1816.

The work is not an original composition but more of an encyclopedia of saints' lives — scores of them. Modern scholars have traced the sources of many of the stories Jacobus tells to earlier works, and they have even been able to discern his critical sensibilities by what he includes and leaves out from other circulating collections and legends. The story of Mary Magdalene, according to Jacobus in *The Golden Legend*, goes like this.

Mary was the sister of Martha and Lazarus. They were part of a wealthy family that owned a great deal of land, including the towns of Magdala and Bethany outright. Lazarus was in the military. Martha, consistent with her busy personality described by Luke (10:38-42), managed the estates. Mary of Magdala, beautiful and wealthy, devoted herself to pleasure of all kinds, including physical.

One day, Mary heard of Jesus, and learned that he was dining at the house of Simon "the leper." She went to him in penitence, and washed his feet with her tears and dried them with her hair — the story told in Luke 7 of a nameless penitent woman. Jacobus identifies the two as one woman, and describes Jesus' act of forgiveness as casting out seven demons.

Mary is now Jesus' devoted disciple.

> "This is the Magdalene upon whom Jesus conferred such great graces and to whom he showed so many marks of love. He cast seven devils out of her, set her totally afire with love of him, counted her among his closest familiars, was her guest, had her do the housekeeping on his travels, and kindly took her side at all times. He defended her when the Pharisee said she was unclean, when her sister implied that she was lazy, when Judas called her wasteful." (*The Golden Legend*, translated by William Granger Ryan [Princeton University Press, 1993], p. 376)

Jacobus then skips many years ahead — fourteen years after the Ascension, to be exact — when the Christian community in Jerusalem was being persecuted. The Resurrection narratives, oddly enough, play no role is his story. Mary, Martha, Lazarus, and others — including a man named Maximin, who was to become, according to the legend, an important bishop — were put in a boat without rudder or sail and set to sea. They ended up in Marseilles, on the southern coast of France.

From this point, the story centers on the astonishing evangelizing career of Mary Magdalene. Her preaching convinces the residents to cease worshiping idols — no wonder, Jacobus remarks, since "the mouth which had pressed such pious and beautiful kisses on the Savior's feet should breathe forth the perfume of the word of God more profusely than others could" (*The Golden Legend*, p. 377).

Mary convinces the governor of Marseilles and his wife of the truth of the Gospel, and they ask her to pray for them to conceive a son. She does, and the wife becomes pregnant. The governor, however, is not quite convinced of the truth of the Gospel, and decides to journey to Rome to speak to Peter himself. (Some suggest that this plot element hints at a discomfort with the charismatically based preaching of a woman, and implies the necessary role of institutional authority.) His wife travels with him, and in the midst of a storm, gives birth and dies.

In a scene somewhat reminiscent of the story of Jonah, the sailors demand that the governor cast his wife's body and newborn son overboard so that the storm will cease. But he refuses, stopping instead to lay them on a hill — the baby on top of its mother's dead body. The ship proceeds to Rome, the governor hears the reassurance he seeks, and is even taken on a side trip to Jerusalem.

On the way back, the governor has a very pleasant surprise: on the shore where he had left them, his son is playing on the beach. The boy runs to his mother's body for protection and to nurse, and at that moment she awakens and tells the governor that Mary Magdalene had protected her and even taken her spirit to Rome and Jerusalem along with him.

Returning to Marseilles, the happy family sees Mary and witness her preaching, and they ask Maximin for baptism, at which point they also lead the destruction of all pagan temples in the city and oversee the election of Lazarus as bishop.

At this point, Jacobus relates, Mary Magdalene retired to the wilderness and "lived unknown for thirty years in a place made ready by the hands of angels" (*The Golden Legend*, p. 380). She was carried to heaven every day during the traditional prayer times, her soul nourished there, and therefore she required no earthly food. She died in a chapel back in the city, after receiving Communion from Bishop Maximin. Jacobus ends his account with stories of miracles attributed to Mary's intercession and her relics, as well as an impatient dismissal of one particular legend that also had currency in the period: that Mary was actually married to John the Evangelist, and it was at their wedding, in Cana, that Jesus had turned water into wine.

The rest of the story, apparently, was that John was inspired to follow Jesus at the wedding, and Mary was so enraged that she gave herself over to sin. Jacobus objects that while the bridegroom at Cana was certainly John (another medieval legend), a reliable report says that the bride in question did not, indeed, react by becoming a sexual libertine, but instead became a companion of the Blessed Virgin, and remained a virgin herself.

"These tales," remarks Jacobus, "are to be considered false and frivolous" (*The Golden Legend*, p. 382).

These, then, are the outlines of the Mary Magdalene legends, as Jacobus relates them. Several other lives of Mary Magdalene dating from the ninth through the thirteenth centuries have been identified, containing some or all of the elements found in Jacobus' account. As we mentioned earlier, the source of the thirty-year period of contemplation is the life of Mary of Egypt, a late fourth- and early fifth-century figure who was reported to have spent fifty years in the desert in Palestine as penance for being a prostitute. Somehow — perhaps because of Mary, the sister of Martha's identity as a contemplative in contrast to her sister — the image came to be associated with Mary Magdalene as well.

Other versions of Mary Magdalene's contemplative life include details drawn from the life of yet another saint: St. Agnes. St. Agnes, thrown naked into a brothel as punishment for refusing the advances of a local Roman official, miraculously saw the hair on her head grow long enough to cover her body. The stories of both Mary of Egypt and Mary Magdalene include miraculous growth of hair, and most artistic depictions of Mary Magdalene in the wilderness present her with hair, cascading from her head, covering her entire body.

We can't really state too strongly how powerful the image of the contemplative Mary Magdalene was to all Christians, no matter the gender. Men, particularly Franciscans and Dominicans, looked to her as a model, as did, in sometimes more radical ways, women who sought to lead lives of solitary contemplation. In Mary Magdalene, they found themselves.

> **"Up to that harsh mountain,**
>
> **Where the Magdalen contemplates,**
>
> **Let us go with sweet songs**
>
> **And a pure and serene mind,**
>
> **She is suspended in the air**
>
> **In the sweet Nazarene face."**
>
> (*Laude*, by Girolamo Savonarola, fifteenth century, cited in Jansen, p. 129)

## Another Life

To get a sense of how rich the medieval reflection on Mary Magdalene was, we'll take a look at one more version of her life. This one, *The Life of St. Mary Magdalene and of Her Sister St. Martha*, has no author attached to it, but the translator and annotator of a recent edition posits that it dates from the late twelfth century and that it reflects the spirituality of St. Bernard of Clairvaux, a renowned preacher and member of the Cistercian monastic order.

St. Bernard's spirituality is marked by a profound, expressive, passionate love. This *Life*, it is suggested, was written by a Cistercian because the author's descriptions of the love Mary had for Jesus are extravagantly passionate, in a way that might sometimes make us, reading it almost a millennium later, uncomfortable.

The scene is like that of *The Golden Legend*: Mary, sister of Martha and Lazarus, is profligate and sensuous. Hearing, though, of Jesus at Simon's house, her conscience is pricked. Drawn by the Holy Spirit, she gathers up her oils and approaches, and in a scene evocative with birth imagery, she is freed from her demons:

> And soon, having by his perpetual interdict driven out and bound up the seven demons which tormented her, he filled her anew with the seven gifts of the Spirit. Impregnated with these, by faith she conceived a good hope within her-

self and gave birth to fervent charity.... With a conscience fruitfully laden with these things and with the fullness of her repentance for her past life, teeming with a devotion pleasing to God, which stirred within her a certain hope of pardon, she came to the supper of the Lord. (*Life*, 35; VI: 230-235)

The *Life* continues, putting Mary at Jesus' side, along with the other women mentioned in Luke 8, and bringing him back to Bethany and Magdala to visit with her family. She is present at many of his miracles, including, of course, the raising of Lazarus. The final anointing at Bethany is described with an acute physicality, and it is worth reading in its entirety:

Having sprinkled the feet of the Savior with the precious nard, she spread it over them and massaged them with her hands and fingers; then she wrapped them gently in her hair, which was of surpassing beauty. Drawing them to her breast and lips, she tenderly washed them. She held them and caressed them for a long time, then let them go.

... After she anointed his feet, there arose in her soul a fire of great love, which he himself had kindled in her, this woman who ministered to him; who, trusting in God and in the affection that had grown between them, performed for him the services of friendship, as she had often, if I'm not mistaken, been allowed to do. Worshiping the Savior, she reverently approached that most holy head which angels, archangels, principalities, and powers venerate. Drawing back with her fingers the hair of Almighty God, she broke the alabaster vessel and poured the remains of the nard over the head of the Son of God. Then, massaging his hair with her hands, she dampened his curls with nard. With her delicate fingers, she skillfully spread the consecrated perfume over his forehead and temples, his neck, and adjacent areas, as though it were the unction of nobility. In this way, Mary fulfilled the works of religious devotion that Solomon in his person once sang of in the Song of Love: "While he was on his couch, my nard gave forth its fragrance." How sweet-smelling were the hands and lips and hair of Mary from the touch of Christ's feet, whose fragrance surpassed all perfumes! Now was the house filled with the scent of the perfume, as the world would be filled with the fame of this deed. (*Life*, 55-56)

The author of the *Life*, in contrast to Jacobus, spends a great deal of time unpacking the four Gospels' accounts of the post-Resurrection appearances, attending closely to the symbolism of the anointing perfumes and the connections to a bride waiting and yearning for her spouse in the Song of Songs. The language is rich and resonant:

At last the Savior was convinced that the love he had before taken such pleasure in had never ceased to burn in the breast of his first servant and special friend, and he knew . . . that he had ascended to the Father in the heart of his perfume-maker. Just as before he had made her the evangelist of his resurrection, so now he made her the apostle of his ascension to the apostles. . . . (*Life*, 72-73)

The author makes, as writers centuries before him had, connections between Mary and Eve:

Behold how the Life, which was lost on earth through Eve, has been restored by him who was brought forth by the Virgin Mary. Just as Eve in paradise had once given her husband a poisoned draught to drink, so now the Magdalene presented to the apostles the chalice of eternal life. (*Life*, 73)

One finds the claim that medieval Christianity demonized Mary (as articulated by writers like Dan Brown in *The Da Vinci*

*Code*) particularly hard to stomach, in light of a summary passage like this:

> The divine honors given her were indeed multiplied, for she was glorified by his first appearance; raised up to the honor of an apostle; instituted as the evangelist of the resurrection of Christ; and designated the prophet of his ascension to his apostles. (*Life*, 79)

The *Life* is quite expressive of that intense Cistercian spirituality that might seem almost erotic to us at times — for example, in this passage describing Mary's sadness after the Ascension, but her eventual comfort in contemplation:

> And finally, after many signs, after long waiting, after hungering for that most happy vision for a long time, she was satisfied with the sight of that beloved face. In the rest of eternal contemplation, he gave her his sweet embraces.... The lover ceaselessly thought of her beloved, and in her meditation she burned with the fire of love, the inextinguishable fire in which she was daily consumed in the holocaust of insatiable desire for her Redeemer. (*Life*, 86-88)

What does this mean? It means, first of all, that the readers of this *Life* were living and listening in a completely different worldview than we are. Salvation, redemption, and eternal life with God who is Love were the fundamental reality for which human beings were created. These people knew of human love, obviously, and they were no strangers to human passion. For them, as for the writer of the Song of Songs a millennium before, the passion between man and woman was not simply an end to itself, and in fact, to treat it as such was sinful. Human love, in its consuming power and life-giving possibility, was a hint of what God's love was about. Many spiritual writers felt absolutely no hesitation in drawing their descriptions of spiritual ecstasy from their knowledge of the ecstasy of human love. What better way to evoke it? What else, in the end, is a better metaphor?

Some modern interpreters see this kind of language as a sign that, indeed, there might have been a deeply buried tradition of a marriage or love affair between Mary Magdalene and Jesus. Not quite, however, for language like this is very closely tied to this particular style of spirituality. And while the Song of Songs imagery of the yearning lover is frequently used to characterize Mary Magdalene, it is also used, in probably more places, to describe the Church in general, waiting for the coming of the Lord.

The fundamental purpose of this language is to reveal to the reader the richness of the love of God, and to inspire him or her to pursue it. Mary, a great sinner, according to this tradition, opened herself to grace, received it, and as fruit, bore within her life the gifts of the Spirit and indefatigable joy. This is not just fruit reserved to her, but to any Christian who loves the Lord with faithfulness and passion:

> ... most happy by far [is] the one who has been so moved by and who has taken such delight in the surpassing fragrance of Mary's deeds that he has followed the example of her conversion, has imprinted in himself the image of her repentance, and has filled his spirit with her devotion, to the degree that he has made himself a partaker of that best part which she chose. (*Life*, 81)

The *Life* then follows Mary, Martha, Lazarus, and Maximin (here called Maximus) to southern France, consistent with the predominant legend at the time. The writer describes Mary's preaching, the power of which was rooted in her conversion and the hope it could give to others, as well as in her intimate knowledge of Jesus:

> ... she showed also the hair with which the first time she dried the drops of her tears from his feet and a second time,

at the feast, she wiped off the precious nard she had poured over those feet; also the mouth together with the lips, by which his feet were kissed thousands and thousands of times, not only while he lived, but also when he was dead and when he had risen from the dead. . . ." (*Life*, 96)

Martha, being the busy one, wasn't sitting still during this time. The *Life* emphasizes her preaching and her miracle-working, especially healing, and both this work and *The Golden Legend* include a story of Martha, somewhat like St. George, defeating a dragon that was terrorizing the populace, subduing it with the Sign of the Cross and by tying her girdle (a type of fabric belt) around its neck.

It is interesting to note that the author of the *Life* knows of the story of Mary Magdalene being taken to heaven seven times daily by angels, but dismisses it with a touch of annoyance, and also dismisses the story of her self-imposed, decades-long exile. He points out that the latter element is taken from the life of the "Penitent of Egypt" — Mary of Egypt — and from those who claim it is found in the works of Josephus; but as he explains, Josephus does not even mention Mary Magdalene. He will allow, however, that the story of the angels might be "understood in a mystical sense," in that Mary certainly contemplated in the presence of angels and was consoled by God in astonishing ways.

Many times, we moderns think of previous generations as being rather charmingly gullible and uncritical. While both Jacobus and the author of the *Life* include stories that might strike us as far-fetched, we can see that actually — working within the context of their own worldviews and sources available, which is all anyone can ever do — they did exercise critical judgment: Jacobus in critiquing the identification of Mary Magdalene with the wedding at Cana, and the *Life*'s author with the stories of Mary in exile. Whether he knew about it or not, it's interesting to note that the *Life*'s author doesn't include the stories about the governor of Marseilles and his wife and child, either.

The *Life* ends, of course, with Mary Magdalene's death. Martha goes first, and only a few days later Mary, sixty-five years old and dying, asks to be taken outdoors. A crowd gathers to pray with her as she awaits her reunion with her Savior. She asks for an account of Jesus' suffering on the cross to be read to her in Hebrew, identified as her native language, and hearing of Jesus' final breath on the cross, she also finally dies.

## Faithful Love

A look at these popular legends about Mary Magdalene reveals a great deal about her appeal during the Middle Ages. She was celebrated, first of all, for her penitence and conversion, and secondly, for her great love of Christ, expressed in her fidelity at the cross. Loving Christ, she in turn is loved and rewarded: she is the first witness at the empty tomb and the "Apostle to the Apostles."

Finally, Mary was a marvel to these people because of her preaching and spiritual life. She was held up as an example and inspiration to sinners everywhere. Mary Magdalene was an extremely popular saint during the Middle Ages precisely because of this. The Blessed Virgin was the object of reverence, too, of course, but what the Magdalene embodied that the Blessed Virgin did not was the dynamic of conversion and the fruit of repentance, so that the hope she held out to the sinner listening to her story was very human, very real, and very possible.

What is fascinating about these accounts is that they contain very few qualifiers related to gender: no implicit criticisms of the perceived weakness of women, no sense of it being unusual to celebrate a woman for her preaching and evangelizing.

It's striking how the popular traditions related to Mary Magdalene were able to see her simply as a beloved and blessed disciple. Their refreshing refusal to be fixated on her "as a woman" in relationship to a world of men is something to note — and, perhaps, to imitate.

## Questions for Reflection

1. What is the portrait of Mary Magdalene that emerges from these legends?

2. Is this portrait in conflict, in spirit, with the portrait in the Gospels?

3. What do you find helpful in these stories? What do you find distracting or not helpful?

## Seven

# TOUCHING THE MAGDALENE

Catholicism is, thank heaven, a faith completely grounded in life — all of it. We believe, quite biblically, that the earth is the Lord's, through which he reveals himself. We don't shy away from physicality, the concrete, or the possibilities of being touched by God through the stuff he has made, including time and space.

Such is the essential meaning of the Incarnation, and it's fundamental to Catholic Christianity. This is the sensibility that lies behind the Catholic use of sacred objects, places, and relics. Just like a letter or a photograph from someone we love, these things can speak eloquently to us of God.

### A Moment in Time

Our celebration of God's work in our lives and in the lives of saints doesn't just happen haphazardly. Human beings dwell in space, and also in time. Christianity, like all other religions, marks time with feasts and seasons, and has done so since the beginning.

The earliest important calendar moments for Christians were, of course, the first day of the week, in honor of the Resurrection, and then, once a year, the Paschal feast, or Easter. The celebrations and rituals surrounding Easter gradually expanded to encompass the Triduum, Holy Week, Lent, and the post-Easter season. The Lord's Nativity was being celebrated in some places by the late fourth century, and the celebration of saints' feast days was well established in the fifth century.

Today, in the Western and most of the Eastern Churches, July 22 is Mary Magdalene's feast day. That date has been constant, and it first appears in a list of saints compiled by the historian Venerable

Bede, from Eastern sources, in the eighth century. Prayers for the feast are found in ninth-century liturgical books, and the complete Mass, with all the prayers and readings composed and arranged in reference to her, is found by the twelfth century (Haskins, p. 109).

The feast of Mary Magdalene was a high-ranking feast as well — a "double," which meant it must be celebrated. The Nicene Creed was recited on her feast day, something that only happened on Sundays and on the feast days of apostles.

In the Western Church, up until the Second Vatican Council, the readings and prayers for July 22 reflected Pope Gregory's conflation of the Marys. When the calendar was revised after the council, references to any other Mary other than the definitively identified Magdalene were removed — the Gospel, for example, is the post-Resurrection encounter between Mary and Jesus in chapter 20 of the Gospel of John, rather than the account of the nameless penitent woman in Luke 7, as it had been for the past thousand years. The liturgies of the Eastern Churches, as we will discuss later, never adapted the Gregorian view, and kept the Marys separate in their commemoration and hagiography.

The date of Mary's feast was made more prominent by celebrations of it in places specifically associated with her, of which there were actually two during the course of the Middle Ages. Both in France, with different claims and convoluted, competitive histories, their stories provide a valuable peek into the role of saints and their relics in medieval Christian life.

### Vézelay

By the early Middle Ages, pilgrims to the Holy Land were visiting the home, or "castle," of Lazarus, Mary Magdalene, and Martha in Bethany, and there were several spots in Jerusalem that were associated with her as the figure conflated with the sinful woman in Luke 7 or with the adulterous woman described in John 8.

Ephesus, too, was strongly associated with Mary Magdalene from antiquity. We will go into more detail on this matter in

Chapter 8 on Eastern Christianity and Mary, but it's worth noting here that many Western writers placed her in Ephesus before the French legends became popular. St. Gregory of Tours, a sixth-century Frankish historian, wrote of Ephesus as Mary's last destination, in which he also included St. John and the Virgin Mary. We have texts reporting on visits to her Ephesus tomb by an eighth-century Anglo-Saxon monk and a twelfth-century Russian, and there is an extensive corpus of legends related to the site in Eastern Christian traditions.

However, in those same early Middle Ages, Christians in the West began to note the presence of Mary Magdalene in their own territories. Relics of Mary Magdalene were claimed as early as the tenth and eleventh centuries in England (a finger) and Spain (some of her hair), and altars were dedicated to her during the same period in a few places throughout Europe.

But the first serious pilgrimage site dedicated to Mary Magdalene was in Vézelay, on a hill in the Burgundy area of France, far away, incidentally, from Marseilles in southern France, where the legends actually placed Mary, Martha, and Lazarus.

Vézelay flourished as a pilgrimage site dedicated to Mary Magdalene, supposedly housing her body, in the twelfth century, encouraged by a determined Abbot Geoffroi. The origins of the *cultus* are, not surprisingly, obscure, but they seem to have begun in the ninth century, when a monk brought some bones to be encased as relics in the church. Historian Christopher Olaf Blum continues the story in the following passage:

> "There they lay in silence for almost a century and a half. In the eleventh century, the cult of Mary Magdalene began to grow in eastern France, where it arrived from Italy via Germany, and churches were dedicated to the saint in Verdun, Reims, and Besançon. Inspired by this growing devotion, Abbot Geoffroi of Vézelay dedicated an altar in the abbey church to the saintly

penitent and encouraged her cult. When a pilgrim from nearby Alésia had her hand healed after praying there, it was noised abroad that the bones in the crypt were the Magdalene's. The monks' initial explanation of how her bones could have found their way from the Holy Land to Burgundy remained the best one: 'all things are possible with God, and whatever he wishes, he does.' " ("Vézelay: The Mountain of the Lord," *Logos: A Journal of Catholic Thought and Culture*, 8:3 [2005], pp. 141-164)

Ultimately, the monks did make attempts to be more specific. In this period before the more generally accepted standardization of *The Golden Legend*, many different accounts of Mary Magdalene's life after the Ascension were still circulating. At first, the Vézelay monks claimed that the body of Mary Magdalene had come to them after one of their monks, Baidilo, made a pilgrimage to the Holy Land and brought the relics from there. A century later, when the Provence legends were gaining in popularity, the explanation was offered that her relics had been taken, or "translated," from Provence and moved north to Burgundy in 745, to protect them from Saracen (Muslim Turkish) invaders. The identity of the relics in Vézelay was formally verified twice, once in the presence of the French king, and the other by a papal legate.

Pilgrimage was a vital spiritual practice during the medieval period. The journey to the holy place was penitential in its physical discomfort, lost wages, and time away from home. The object of pilgrimage contained relics or had been the location of an important event, such as a vision, a miracle, or a martyrdom. Vézelay, as the location of the relics of the penitent Mary Magdalene, was a place where Christians came to have their sins forgiven and be healed of their ailments. So many former prisoners — freed, they believed, because of her intercession — laid their chains down before her relics that the abbot was able to melt the chains and forge an altar rail from them. Vézelay's popularity was aided by its location on one of the pilgrimage routes to Santiago de Compostela in Spain (still a well-traversed pilgrimage route), and in turn, it fed the popularity of St. Mary Magdalene, her legend, and her feast day.

This was not to last, however, and the history of Vézelay turned out to be a difficult one. Rivalries between monks and townspeople, and between French nobility and Rome, all worked to weaken the monastery. The questions that had always lurked as to the identity of the relics loomed even larger as, in the thirteenth century, the tales of Mary Magdalene in Provence began to take hold in the popular mind, and more sites in that area became associated with her.

In 1295, Pope Boniface VIII declared that her body lay in Aix, near Marseilles, not in Vézelay, and the glory days of the monastery were over. The church, newly built in the twelfth century, was defaced during the French Revolution, as were so many churches in France, but was restored in the mid-nineteenth century. Sadly, most of the original art and architectural features depicting Mary Magdalene no longer exist.

### Saint-Maximin

Since the thirteenth century, the center of the Mary Magdalene cult has been in Saint-Maximin, in southern France. In the early part of the century, a grotto in the mountains near the town had come to be identified and revered as the spot where she spent those last contemplative years of her life, and this was even acknowledged in the accounts written about the theft of her relics by the monks of Vézelay.

For an unknown reason, in 1279, the monks of another monastery — in Saint-Maximin — put out the word that they had discovered Mary Magdalene's body in their own church. The marble sarcophagus, dating from the fourth century and of Roman design, was said to contain the body of a woman, with either (depending on the account) a fennel or a palm growing out the skull's mouth — the palm symbolizing her evangelizing. Claims were made of dated documents from the eighth century attesting to the woman's identity as Mary Magdalene. The explanation was that the monks in charge back then had buried the relics, once again, to protect them from the Saracens. In 1295, Pope Boniface VIII authenticated the relics and placed the Dominicans, who adopted Mary as one of their patrons, in charge, which they still are to this day.

In 1315, Saint-Maximin produced what could be seen as final proof of the authenticity of its claim: a *Book of Miracles of St. Mary Magdalene*. As historian Katherine Ludwig Jansen makes clear, the book was a double-edged sword, being not simply a celebration of Mary Magdalene, but a pointed slap at Vézelay: the first miracle recorded in the book described a contrast between the powerlessness of the Vézelay relics and the miraculous power of those in Provence (Jansen, p. 43).

Mary Magdalene is still celebrated in Saint-Maximin today. The grotto of her purported contemplative career is still a pilgrimage site. It is located high on a mountain called Ste-Baume, accessible after a forty-five-minute walk from the Benedictine convent that provides lodgings to pilgrims. Her relics, back in the village, are brought out on her feast day of July 22. A head-shaped reliquary contains a skull and, carried by twelve men, is processed through the village of Saint-Maximin, while villagers dressed in thirteenth-century garb join in.

There are ways to reconcile all of the legends. Older Catholic books do this by saying that a Vézelay monk did, indeed, take relics from Saint-Maximin to protect them from the Saracens, leaving some behind (those that were then rediscovered in the thirteenth century). However, the popularity of the Saint-Maximin relics and the collapse of the Vézelay shrine tell us what the sense of the faithful on the matter was. It made perfect sense to them to honor Mary Magdalene in the place where she was supposed to have lived, preached, prayed, and passed on to God.

## Questions for Reflection

1. What is the purpose of pilgrimage?
2. What objects, places, and times do you associate with faith?
3. Why were Mary Magdalene's relics important to these shrines?

## Eight

# TO THE EAST

The legendary material about Mary Magdalene coming out of the Western Christian tradition is rich enough in its own right. The figure of the penitent, preaching, and contemplative Mary was a powerful and popular one in medieval Christianity.

Western Christianity, predominantly shaped by Western European worldviews, is only part of the Christian picture, however. There is a whole other, yet closely linked world out there: that of the Christian Churches of the East, rooted in apostolic Tradition, and embodied in Eastern Orthodoxy and the Eastern rites of the Catholic Church.

When we speak of Eastern Christian tradition, we are speaking of national Churches centered in the Middle East, Africa, and Eastern Europe. They trace their roots back to apostolic times and share six hundred years of theological tradition with the West. Because of cultural, linguistic, spiritual, and theological distinctions, the traditions really began to diverge after the sixth century, particularly as Western Christianity extended into Europe and began to adapt to the cultural landscape and needs of the Germanic tribes. A formal schism occurred in 1054.

The Eastern Orthodox Churches are completely separate from Catholicism. They do see the pope as a legitimate bishop, although they do not hold to the Roman interpretation of what the "primacy" of the bishop of Rome might mean.

Eastern-rite Churches, often confused with Orthodoxy by Westerners, are Churches that are in communion with Rome and are under the authority of the pope. They are Catholic Churches, but with an external and internal life that resembles Orthodoxy more than it does, say, a typical Latin-rite Catholic parish in the United States.

To these Christians, too, Mary Magdalene is a saint. But at this point, much like the traditions of East and West as a whole, the streams diverge.

### 'Myrrh-bearer'

To put it most simply, the Eastern view of Mary Magdalene, although marked by some unique legendary material, in general cleaves much more closely to what the Gospels tell us about her. The East never adopted St. Gregory the Great's conflation of the Marys, and their commemoration of Mary Magdalene on her feast day has always been centered on her role as witness to the empty tomb and her declaration, "He is risen!"

The title with which Mary is honored in Eastern Christianity, while unwieldy to English speakers, makes this association clear. She is called "Myrrh-bearer" (she is also known as "Equal-to-the-Apostles," or *Isapostole*, and by the term mentioned earlier, "Apostle to the Apostles"). As a myrrh-bearer, she is also honored in Orthodoxy on the second Sunday after Easter (Pascha), the "Sunday of the Myrrh-bearing Women," along with seven other women who are mentioned by the Gospel writers as having an important role at the cross or at the tomb:

> "You did command the myrrh-bearers to rejoice, O Christ!
> By your resurrection, you did stop the lamentation of Eve,
>     O God!
> You did command your apostles to preach: The Savior is
>     risen!"
>
> (Kontakion, Sunday of the Myrrh-bearing Women)

Two weeks before, on Pascha itself, it is traditional to sing a hymn in honor of Mary Magdalene, one written, intriguingly, by a woman.

Kassia, the composer of this hymn, was born in Constantinople in the ninth century. She married and had children, but eventually established and led a monastery in that city. She is believed to have composed more than fifty hymns, thirty of which are still in use in the Orthodox liturgy today. She also wrote secular poetry, and she was the author of a number of pithy epigrams ("Love everyone, but don't trust all" is one of many).

Her troparion, or short praise-hymn, puts us in the heart of Mary Magdalene as she approaches the tomb:

> "Sensing your divinity, Lord,
> a woman of many sins
> takes it upon herself
> to become a myrrh-bearer
> and in deep mourning
> brings before you fragrant oil
> in anticipation of your burial; crying:
> "Woe to me! What night falls on me,
> what dark and moonless madness
> of wild desire, this lust for sin.
> Take my spring of tears
> you who draw water from the clouds,
> bend to me, to the sighing of my heart,
> you who bend the heavens
> in your secret incarnation,
> I will wash your immaculate feet with kisses
> and wipe them dry with the locks of my hair;
> those very feet whose sound Eve heard
> at the dusk in Paradise and hid herself in terror.
> Who shall count the multitude of my sins
> or the depth of your judgment,
> Savior of my soul?
> Do not ignore your handmaiden,
> you whose mercy is endless."

What is clear in this hymn is that despite the Eastern determination to keep the different women straight, the pull of the symbolism of anointing is too great to resist. The "demons" that Luke and Mark describe are characterized as "sins," which then evokes the penitent woman in Luke 7, just as it did in Western tradition.

Mary Magdalene's feast itself is celebrated in most Eastern Christian Churches, as it is in the West, on July 22 — although in various parts of the East, her feast is noted on June 30 or August 4. (Mary of Bethany, by the way, is remembered on June 4.) In addition, the East has traditionally remembered Mary Magdalene on yet another day: the occasion of the translation of her relics from Ephesus to Constantinople, under the ninth-century emperor Leo VI, on May 4.

The prayers for the July 22 celebration — from the liturgy, Vespers and Matins — make clear the point of reverence the East has for Mary Magdalene:

"When Christ appeared, you followed in his footsteps, holy Myrrh-bearer all-praised, and served him most ardently with upright intent; nor did you abandon him in death, but you went, and with compassion brought him sweet spices with your tears. Therefore we keep the festival of your all-holy memory." (Vespers)

"Mary Magdalene, having as his disciple faithfully served Christ our God, who willingly made himself poor with my poverty in his surpassing compassion, when she saw him stretched on a cross and shut up in a tomb, weeping cried out, 'What is this strange sight? How is he who gives life to the dead numbered among the dead? What sweet spices can I bring the one who freed me from the foul stench of the demons? What tears can I shed for the one who stripped my foremother of her tears?' But the Sovereign of the universe, appearing like the

> guardian of Paradise, by the dew of his words banished the heat and said to her, 'Go to my brethren and shout aloud the good tidings of joy: I am ascending to my Father and your Father, and my God and your God, that I may grant the world my great mercy.' " (Vespers)

The prayers for Matins reflect the long-perceived connection between Eve and Mary Magdalene:

> "The foremother, seeing the one who tricked her by words and exiled her from Paradise of old trampled on by holy women who had gained a will of courage, rejoices with them eternally.
>
> "Wounded with longing for his sweet love, you bring sweet spices to the one who breathes life into all, now slain and lying in a tomb, holy Mary Magdalen, and pour out the fragrant scent of tears.
>
> "After the divine Passion, after the dread Resurrection of the Savior, you hurried to and fro, proclaiming the holy word, and as a Disciple of the Word catching many who had been deceived by ignorance, glorious Saint." (Matins)

After the Ascension, the apostles scattered in order to fulfill Jesus' mandate to go out, preach, and baptize all nations. Mary Magdalene, as we've noted, was understood to have carried forth that mandate as well, bringing the Gospel to southern France, according to the West. The East celebrates Mary's evangelizing efforts as well, but tells a different story of where she went in his name.

## To Ephesus

Rome and Ephesus are the two points where Eastern traditions place Mary Magdalene. Her purported presence in Rome has actually given rise to one of the more enduring symbols associated with her, aside from her ointment jar: the red egg.

The story goes that Mary went to Rome to preach the Gospel, and while there she met with the emperor Tiberius. For some reason — perhaps because, as one tradition holds, the meeting was at a dinner — Mary was holding an egg in her hand, and while doing so proclaimed to the emperor that "Christ is risen!" This was consistent with her role as witness to the Risen Lord. Tiberius laughed, and said that a man could rise from the dead just as easily as the egg in her hand could turn red. Which, of course, it promptly did. In Orthodox churches, the tradition persists of sharing red eggs on Pascha, and some Easter European and Russian cultures are known for elaborately designed eggs for the season.

But Mary was not done with the emperor. As she continued to share the story of Jesus with him, she let him know that it was Pontius Pilate, the governor of Judea, who had been responsible for the execution of the Risen One, prompting, the story concludes, with the emperor sending Pilate to Gaul, effectively in exile, where he died. Most traditions do, indeed, put Pilate in Europe at the time of his death, and some indicate that he committed suicide. Eastern Orthodoxy recognizes his wife, Procula, who tried to dissuade him from allowing Jesus' execution, as a saint.

Some Eastern traditions maintain that Mary stayed in Rome until Paul arrived, and interpret the Mary praised by Paul in Romans 16:6, as one "who has worked hard among you," as Mary Magdalene.

Eastern Christianity uniformly places Mary Magdalene in Ephesus, a city on the western coast of Turkey by the end of her life. The city exists now only in ruins, but they are extensive, well-preserved ruins that are a popular pilgrimage and tourist destination. Mary was in the city, it is said, in the company of John the Evangelist, and some threads of tradition say that besides evangelizing the area, she helped him write his Gospel there. Modestus, a seventh-century patriarch of Jerusalem, noted the following:

"After the death of Our Lord, the Mother of God and Mary Mag-dalene joined John, the well-beloved disciple, at Ephesus. It is there that the myrrhophore ended her apostolic career through her martyrdom, not wishing to the very end to be separated from John the apostle and the Virgin." (Quoted in Haskins, p. 104)

When Mary Magdalene died, she was buried at the mouth of a cave that eventually became known as the Cave of the Seven Sleepers — a grotto in which seven young Christian men had been buried alive during the reign of Emperor Decius in the third century. Two hundred years later, it is said, the cave was opened and the seven youths were found to have been only sleeping. Mary's body remained there until the ninth century, when Emperor Leo the Wise ordered it moved to Constantinople, to a monastery called St. Lazarus.

At this point, the story of her relics — for in Christianity, a saint's life never ends with physical death, as the story of their bodies becomes a way to tell the bigger Christian story — coincides with parts of the Western traditions. Some Eastern traditions do say that her relics were sent to St. John Lateran in Rome in the midst of the Crusades. One of the many monasteries on Mount Athos in Greece, Simonas Petras, claims to have one of Mary Magdalene's hands, which, some pilgrims report even today, is warm to the touch.

### 'Equal-to-the-Apostles'

Mary Magdalene may be honored in Eastern Christianity by this title above all, but she is not the only woman that Orthodoxy honors in this way. Various parts of the Orthodox world honor a few other women as *Isapostole*: Photini, the name given to the Samaritan woman at the well, whom Jesus meets in John 4, and who goes out to evangelize her own people; Apphia, the wife of Philemon (the owner of the slave Onesimus), to whom Paul wrote one of his letters; Marianne, purportedly the sister of Philip and Bartholomew; Thecla, whose life is described from an apocryphal work associating her with Paul; Nino, a fourth-century evangelizer of the Georgian people; Helena, the mother of Emperor Constantine; and Olga, a tenth-century Russian queen, who is credited with preparing the soil of Russia for conversion to Christianity through her own witness.

All of these women — and a few men — are considered by Eastern Christians to be "Equal-to-the-Apostles." But Mary Magdalene is revered as preeminent among them for her evangelizing, rooted in her gratitude to Jesus, her deep love for him, and her profound experience of the Risen Lord, which moved her to proclaim the Good News that Christ is risen.

It was Pope John Paul II who pointed out the necessity of the Christian world breathing "with both lungs" — that is, living the faith and worshiping the Lord with an appreciation for the sensibilities of both Eastern and Western Christianity. In the East's emphasis on Mary Magdalene as witness to the empty tomb and "Equal-to-the-Apostles," as she preached the Good News, we see the truth of this observation: for while at times Western Christianity has, if not forgotten, at least deemphasized this fundamental, scripturally rooted understanding of Mary Magdalene, the East, despite its own legendary accretions, has preserved it largely intact, and kept it as the focal point of their devotion to her, "Myrrh-bearer" and "Equal-to-the-Apostles."

### Questions for Reflection

1. What are some of the legends related to Mary Magdalene that came from the East?
2. What strikes you as most meaningful about the East's devotion to Mary Magdalene?

## Nine

# THE PENITENT

Saints are dynamic figures in Christian tradition. Their popularity waxes and wanes, depending on the needs of a given era. The more popular saints, whose lives are particularly rich and evocative, end up being many things to many people.

St. Francis of Assisi is a good example. The thirteenth-century friar is revered by animal lovers, Church reformers, advocates for traditional piety, peace activists, those who serve the poor, and even gardeners. Under all the layers of devotion and interpretation, one finds a man on fire with the love of Christ, completely open to God's will, an aspect which all the agenda-driven advocates tend to ignore.

Mary Magdalene, as we've seen already, fits into this paradigm. The huge gaps in our knowledge of her lend themselves to myth-making and legend-weaving. In addition, the themes of her life have resonated with Christians on many levels, in different periods and cultures. By the High Middle Ages and through the Baroque period — from about the fourteenth through the eighteenth centuries — the image of Mary Magdalene that dominated Christian thinking in the West was that of penitent.

### Sin and Repentance

As we've seen, Mary Magdalene is never explicitly identified as a "sinner" in the Gospels. The connection was made in the early centuries of Christianity, mostly because of the confusion about what her "seven demons" could mean and the not-surprising association of her possessed state with that of the "sinful woman" mentioned in Luke 7, mere verses before we are introduced to Mary Magdalene by name. While medieval legends that emphasized her role in evangelizing southern France continued to be popular through the Middle Ages, the image that really took hold in the popular consciousness was, indeed, that of Mary Magdalene as a once sinful, now repentant woman.

Why?

Some contemporary writers would have us believe that it is all about the repression of women, about demonizing Mary Magdalene in order to minimize her contribution to Christianity as "Apostle to the Apostles," and perhaps even to hide some ancient memory of her leadership role in early Christianity.

Such a view may be intriguingly conspiratorial, but fortunately (or unfortunately, depending on your point of view) it has no basis in historical reality. As even our rather cursory study should make clear, the sources of Christian thinking about Mary Magdalene through that first millennium aren't exactly linear, and they don't emerge from some sort of Central Control, directing the image that must prevail, else women get uppity.

To be sure, Mary Magdalene imagery does not exist in a vacuum — which is actually our greater point here — and does, indeed, reflect cultural norms and expectations about women, sin, and sexuality. But here, as always, context is everything. It is all well and good to examine the image of the repentant Mary Magdalene for what it tells us about late medieval expectations of women and sexuality, but what's ignored in those discussions is, first of all, that she was not presented as an example just for women, but for all people.

> "For through her example, she is instruction for us. She teaches what we sinners ought to do. She did not despair, she did not presume, she did not deny her sins, she did not ignore them, but rather with bitter laments and tears, having cast off all human shame, she sought forgiveness." (Eudes de Cateauroux, cited in Jansen, p. 231)

Furthermore, while Mary Magdalene might have been the most powerful symbol of repentance in this era, she was not the only one. The apostle Peter, of course, was remembered in the same way — without the sexual aspect, of course. But there are, for example, a number of artistic representations of Mary Magdalene as repentant sinner that are part of a pair, the other piece being Peter, sorrowful over his denial of Jesus. Those who like to attribute Mary's popularity as sinner to a deeply felt desire of patriarchal Church leaders to demean her, her leadership, and all women, might consider the emphasis on Peter's sin, which was, of course, actually far more serious and actually specifically mentioned in Scripture. Is the emphasis on Peter reflective of a desire to diminish him or his role in Church history? In this era — the late Middle Ages and Renaissance, when the papacy was at the height of its power — that seems highly unlikely.

Why any particular angle on the Christian story gains ascendance in an era is not a question that can ever be answered with absolute certainty, and never simply. The medieval Christian worldview emphasized penance and the possibility of redemption. Europe was devastated by plague during this time, a tragedy that is estimated to have killed one-third of Europe's population, and was widely believed to have been sent by God as chastisement. As European economies progressed, greater wealth led to greater profligacy. Medieval people certainly did not harbor idealistic illusions about humanity, but the widespread corruption in Church institutions, much remarked on in the years leading up to the Reformation, made its mark as well, highlighting the constancy of human sin.

In addition, Church practices regarding penance continued to develop in ways that profoundly impacted the ordinary Christian.

In earliest Christianity, baptism was generally a ritual for adults who had been through intensive preparation called the catechumenate. Sins that were committed after baptism were considered quite serious, and they brought on what we would see as harsh penance — confession of one's sin, usually to the local bishop, would bring on de facto excommunication for a period of months or even years, depending on the offense. Such was the shape of what we call the Sacrament of Reconciliation in the earliest years of Christianity.

By the early Middle Ages — the sixth and seventh centuries — infant baptism had become more and more common, and it was even the norm in some areas. In that context, penance took on a rather different shape in people's lives. It was no longer the ritual for confessing the most serious violations of Christian life in the context of a baptism that had been freely chosen, after intensive preparation as an adult. It became a means for Christians, baptized as infants, to reconcile themselves with God and the Church, in matters great and small.

This way of experiencing the sacrament was institutionalized and normalized in the early Middle Ages, culminating the Fourth Lateran Council in 1215, which, in its Canon 21, made yearly confession of one's sins to a priest mandatory.

It was in this environment that the image of the penitent Magdalene took hold in the popular imagination: a culture highly aware of sin, mortality, and eternal consequences — and a Church that was giving renewed and vigorous emphasis to the Sacrament of Reconciliation. She functioned as a model for repentance and its fruit.

> "Happy Maria,
> Hope of forgiveness,
> Model of penance,
> Mirror of conversion
> Who pleased the Lord for us."
>
> (Fifteenth-century hymn from Marseilles, quoted in Jansen, p. 233)

### An Inspiration to Penitents

One of the most vivid ways we see Mary Magdalene's inspiration to medieval penitents is through her patronage of penitential societies.

Medieval ways of doing penance were often public and could be extreme. This goes back to the early Church, when penitents were sometimes instructed, for example, to don sackcloth and ashes and sit outside the church, which they were prohibited from entering.

In the extreme and dramatic era of medieval Christianity, in a culture in which violence was a normal mode of problem solving, physically austere and even painful means of reparation for sin were not unusual — not that these kinds of penances were actually given to lay people by the priests to whom they confessed. They were, however, known, used in religious orders, and adopted by laity, who even organized themselves into groups in the name of penance. In the wake of the Black Death, these groups became even more prominent, as the sense grew that radical, communal action needed to be taken in order to stay God's hand from inflicting further punishment.

These groups, called *disciplinati,* or more popularly, "flagellants," actually did engage in very public self-flogging in a highly ritualized manner, and were generally barely tolerated or even discouraged by local bishops. Several of them adopted Mary Magdalene as their patron saint, fixing her image on their banners. They gathered for special liturgies on feasts of the Blessed Virgin, the apostles, and Mary Magdalene. The members of one group had to give special reverence to images of Mary Magdalene. One striking banner for one of the groups depicts a towering figure of Mary Magdalene, holding her ointment jar and a crucifix, surrounded by angels and, at her feet, four quite small, kneeling, shrouded penitents, whose robes were open in the back, showing their wounds (Jansen, pp. 227-228).

Another means of encouraging repentance among medieval Christians, and one that was far more institutionally respectable, was through the mendicant orders. The Franciscans and Dominicans, established in the thirteenth century, were reform orders that emphasized, among other activities like service to the poor and preaching, the necessity and fruit of repentance.

The Dominicans adopted Mary Magdalene as their patroness in the late thirteenth century — but, in reality, she was adopted *for them* by the actions of Charles II, king of Naples and count of Provence. The story of how this happened takes us back to the now-familiar road to Saint-Maximin.

After the relics of Mary Magdalene were rediscovered and authenticated at Saint-Maximin, someone had to be put in charge of the shrine. Charles, perhaps inspired by the recent innovation of establishing orders of penitents, usually prostitutes — some under the auspices of the Dominicans — determined that it would be St. Dominic's order that would care for the shrine. Encouraged by the pope, the order moved into the shrine in 1295. In 1297, her feast was celebrated throughout the order for the first time, and her patronage was secure.

The Dominicans maintained a presence at the shrine for five hundred years, until the French Revolution, and fifty years later it was another Dominican, Jean-Baptiste Henri Lacordaire, who saw to the reclamation and reconstruction of Saint-Maximin. Mary Magdalene is often present with St. Dominic in religious art from the period, highlighting her importance as the penitent patron of the order that was established to preach reform and penitence. As one Dominican scholar has written, "The body of the Magdalene is guarded by the Preachers; the Order of Preachers is guarded by the Magdalene" ("Mary Magdalene: The Apostle of the Apostles and the Order of Preachers," by Guy Bedouelle, O.P., *Dominican Ashram*, Vol. 18, No. 4, 1999, pp. 157-171).

In her book *The Making of the Magdalen*, Katherine Ludwig Jansen examines in great detail the important role the saint played in the preaching of the mendicant orders. The Franciscans and Dominicans, even with their approved rules, often operated under suspicion from local clergy. Mary Magdalene, a woman preaching, also an outsider of sorts, was a model for them, as was she in her legendary rejection of her wealth and her mix of the contemplative and the active life.

## Magdalenes

One of the most direct connections between Mary Magdalene and penitence was made, in the Middle Ages and beyond, through the foundation of establishments for prostitutes, under her patronage. One of the most successful was the Penitent Sisters of Blessed Mary Magdalene, established by Rudolph of Worms, in Germany, in the thirteenth century.

The story goes that Rudolph was on his way to a preaching mission when he met a group of prostitutes who begged him for help. Those for whom he could not find husbands (actually a common first recourse in trying to assist prostitutes during this period) he brought into convents. The order was given papal sanction and placed under the rule (or way of life) of St. Augustine, and it spread rapidly. Rather than being a full-fledged religious order as we think of it, it was more of a halfway house, in which women who wished to escape prostitution could reclaim their lives.

> **Prostitution was legally and socially tolerated through most of Europe in the medieval period. Some municipalities had organized legal brothels, and many regulated the locations where prostitution could be practiced and what clothes prostitutes could wear. In the fifteenth century, in one region of France, as a part of a fair, prostitutes competed in a footrace that was held on July 22 (Haskins, p. 168).**

This group, popularly referred to as the "White Ladies," spread rapidly, and was followed by the establishment of similar groups and houses, also under the patronage of St. Mary Magdalene, across Europe. The inspiration did not cease with the Middle Ages, however. Institutions for prostitutes and other women finding themselves in difficult situations continued to be established through the nineteenth century.

In 1618, Père Athanase Molé, a Capuchin, founded the Order of St. Mary Magdalene in France, which was divided into three parts: the Magdalenes, who took solemn vows; the Sisters of St. Martha, who took only simple vows, and therefore had a more flexible relationship to the community; and finally the Sisters of St. Lazarus, who were, in the words of the 1918 *Catholic Encyclopedia*, "public sinners confined against their will." The order no longer exists.

Christians established ways to help many in need besides prostitutes under the patronage of St. Mary Magdalene. During the Middle Ages, sixty-three hospitals were dedicated to her in England alone, along with many others in France and Italy. The association of Mary Magdalene with these corporal works of mercy is most deeply rooted in her role of caring for Jesus' dead body. Many leper hospitals operated under her patronage, perhaps because of the confusion of her purported brother Lazarus with a leprous beggar with that name in one of Jesus' parables (Luke 16:20; Jansen, pp. 111-113).

St. Mary Euphrasia Pelletier founded another French-based Magdalene order in the nineteenth century. Some of the more well-known and notorious institutions in this category are, of course, the Irish-based "Magdalene asylums."

The Magdalene movement of assisting girls and women took on new life in the nineteenth century, as industrialization and urbanization produced a large number of displaced women who turned to prostitution, or were simply destitute. In Ireland, the job of providing shelter for these women was taken up by the Church, most notably the Sisters of Mercy. In the early days, the Magdalene institutions were relatively open, centered on laundry as a primary work activity, and women moved in and out of the houses as the need demanded. However, over time, they became more prison-like, with environments that became abusive. The terrible conditions in some of these houses were exposed in Ireland in the 1970s, dramatized in a 2002 film called *The Magdalene Sisters*. The Sisters of Mercy issued a formal apology for the order's historical mistreatment of residents of their Magdalene asylums in 1996.

## Forgiveness and Hope

It is a long way from Luke's grace-filled moment between Jesus and the penitent woman to the harsh abuse of the Magdalene asylums. As is the case too often with religious imagery, the figure of the repentant Magdalene, which should be a symbol of hope, was turned into an overseer, at least nominally, of hopelessness. It is a warning to us to be ever-vigilant, lest the light that shines so clearly in the Gospel — in this case, of the grace of God's forgiveness and love — be subsumed into the social structures of our own time, so that rather than being a way to God, our actions work as an obstacle instead.

### Questions for Reflection

1. Why were Christians in the Middle Ages so aware of the need for penance in their lives?
2. How did Mary Magdalene give hope to people in the Middle Ages?

# Ten

# MARY AND THE MYSTICS

The heart of the Christian life is prayer, and throughout our history Mary Magdalene has often been found in that heart, pointing the way to Christ. Like any saint, Christians have looked to her as a model, and have prayed for her intercession.

In this chapter, we'll look at some important figures in the Christian spiritual tradition, mostly women, and how they have been inspired and nourished by the example of Mary Magdalene. Some found parallels between their lives and hers. Others found strength in her identity as a repentant sinner, or in the model of solitary contemplation offered by the legends they knew. The lives of all of these prayerful people help us see the tremendous positive power the figure of Mary Magdalene has held in the lives of many Christians.

## Like a Sister

Margery Kempe is one of the more vivid figures to emerge from the medieval period, partly because she left extensive autobiographical writings (dictated to a priest), but also because her experiences are so extreme to the point that today we might indeed diagnose her as mentally ill.

She was an Englishwoman, born in the late thirteenth century, married, and the mother of fourteen children. She eventually convinced her husband to live with her as a brother, and from that point embarked on a number of pilgrimages — to the Holy Land, Rome, Santiago de Compostela, Norway, and Germany. Her *Book of Margery Kempe* is an invaluable record of the period in general, and of religious life and sensibilities in particular.

The *Book* records visionary experiences, most of which involve Margery, who refers to herself as "said creature," in the midst of a biblical scene, observing and interacting with the other partici-pants, often weeping copiously. Her visions reflect a knowledge of some of the medieval religious plays featuring Mary Magdalene, as well as a work called *Meditations on the Life of Christ*, a very pop-ular devotional believed to have been written by St. Bonaventure, but now ascribed to a figure known as "Pseudo-Bonaventure."

Margery joins Mary Magdalene and others at the cross. She mourns with them. For ten years, on every Good Friday, she weeps for five or six hours. After the Resurrection, she displaces Mary Magdalene, and converses with Christ herself, receiving his assur-ance that if Mary Magdalene could be forgiven of her sins, so should Margery. She, along with the Virgin, expresses sorrow at the imminent physical departure of Jesus, and is comforted by him.

Margery draws strength from Mary Magdalene, then, as a model of a sinner who loved Christ and was devoted to him. The imagery she offers, of herself mourning over the dead Christ, kiss-ing his feet and caring for his body, is evocative of spiritual writ-ing and art of the period in which Mary Magdalene is playing that same role:

> [Jesus to Margery Kempe:] "Also, daughter, I know . . . how you call Mary Magdalene into your soul to welcome me for, daugh-ter, I know well enough what you are thinking. You think that she is the worthiest, in your soul, and you trust most in her prayers next to my mother, and so you may indeed, daughter, for she is a very great mediator to me for you in the bliss of heaven." (*Book of Margery Kempe*, chapter 86, in *Medieval Writings on Female Spirituality*, edited by Elizabeth Spearing [Penguin Books, 2002], p. 251)

### The Second Mary Magdalene

Similar comfort was found by St. Margaret Cortona (1247-1297), who is actually called the "Second Mary Magdalene." She was born in Tuscany, and as a young adult woman she became lovers with a nobleman, bore him a child, and lived with him for nine years. The man was murdered, at which point Margaret took her child and fled, first to her family's home, where she was rejected, and then to a Franciscan friary. Her subsequent life as a Franciscan tertiary was marked by continued battles with temptations of the flesh (she is a patron saint of those battling temptation), repentance, and service to the poor.

Obviously, her past life led to her identification with the popular memory of St. Mary Magdalene, repentant sinner — and like Margery Kempe, Margaret found solace in Mary's penitent life. The following was related by one of her early biographers:

> "Shortly before her death, she had a vision of St. Mary Magdalene, 'most faithful of Christ's apostles, clothed in a robe as it were of silver, and crowned with a crown of precious gems, and surrounded by the holy angels.' And whilst she was in this ecstasy Christ spoke to Margaret, saying: 'My Eternal Father said of Me to the Baptist: This is My beloved Son; so do I say to thee of Magdalene: This is my beloved daughter.' On another occasion we are told that 'she was taken in spirit to the feet of Christ, which she washed with her tears as did Magdalene of old; and as she wiped His feet she desired greatly to behold His face, and prayed to the Lord to grant her this favor.' Thus to the end we see she was the same; and yet the difference." (*Saints for Sinners*, by Alban Goodier, S.J. [Ignatius Press, 1993], p. 46)

## Bathed in Blood

St. Catherine of Siena is one of the most fascinating women of the medieval period, and considering the competition, that is saying quite a bit.

Born in 1347, the youngest of twenty-five children, Catherine was intensely devout, but uninterested in taking the usual route for young women like herself, which would have been joining a religious community. She became associated with the Dominicans — whose patron was Mary Magdalene, remember — as a tertiary, but operated with a startling degree of independence for a woman of her era. We remember her today for her letters, her spiritual writings (dictated to her confessor, Blessed Raymond of Capua), and her determination to play a role in reforming the papacy, at that time in exile in Avignon, France, and corrupted by luxury.

Catherine saw Mary Magdalene as a second mother, having dedicated herself to her in a special way upon the death in childbirth of her sister, Bonaventura, an incident that seems to have been an important motivator in Catherine's spiritual life. When Bonaventura died, Catherine envisioned herself at the feet of Christ, with Mary Magdalene, begging for mercy. Her biographer noted Catherine "doing everything she could to imitate her to obtain forgiveness" (quoted in Haskins, p. 179). Blessed Raymond summarizes Catherine's devotion in the following passage:

> "'Sweetest daughter, for your greater comfort I give you Mary Magdalen for your mother. Turn to her in absolute confidence; I entrust her with a special care of you.' The virgin gratefully accepted this offer. . . . From that moment the virgin felt entirely at one with the Magdalen and always referred to her as her mother." (Quoted in Jansen, p. 303)

In terms of her personal spirituality, Catherine looked to Mary Magdalene as a model of repentance and faithfulness, never leaving Jesus at the cross. Nor, she determined, would she, faithfully persevering in fidelity despite the extraordinary risks she faced in confronting the most powerful figure of the day — the pope — with evidence of his own sins.

[Catherine of Siena on Mary Magdalene, the "loving disciple":] "Wracked with love, she runs and embraces the cross. There is no doubt that to see her master, she becomes inundated with blood." (Quoted in Haskins, p. 188)

## St. Teresa of Ávila

The sixteenth century was a period of conflict and reform for the Catholic Church. At the beginning of the century, there was only one Christian Church in the West, but by the end there were scores of different churches and movements emanating from the Protestant Reformation.

The Catholic Church, faced with the consequences of, in part, its own weakness and corruption, responded to the Reformation with its own inner purification, commonly called the Counter-Reformation, or the Catholic Reformation. The Council of Trent, meeting over several years mid-century, standardized prayer and liturgical texts, mandated seminary training for priests, and confidently restated traditional Catholic teaching on justification, Scripture, Tradition, and the life of the Church.

Change doesn't come only from the top, though. When a reforming spirit is in the Catholic air, inevitably groups rise up to meet the challenge and undertake the work. It happened, for example, in the thirteenth century with the rise of the mendicant orders. Some argue it is happening today with the rising popularity of groups like Communion and Liberation, Opus Dei, and the Neo-Catechumenal Way.

The sixteenth century was no different. It was the era that saw the establishment of the Jesuits, who evangelized with vigor and focus, under the direct supervision of the pope. It was also the era that saw the reformation of many religious orders. One of the most important leaders on this score was St. Teresa of Ávila, who worked tirelessly to reform the Carmelites in Spain.

Not that she started out life as a reformer. Teresa entered religious life at an early age, but did not pursue holiness with much vigor. Many convents in that period had devolved to essentially groups of well-off women living together, living only nominally religious lives.

Teresa lived this way until her forties, when illness prompted a change of heart. In the wake of her conversion, Teresa was inspired to reform existing houses of her order and establish new ones that would be expressions of a sacrificial road to holiness. Teresa was also a great mystic and teacher of prayer. Her works — including her *Life*, the *Way of Perfection*, and *The Interior Castle* — are still widely read today.

In these works, we see the influence of Mary Magdalene on Teresa, primarily, as she has been for the other women we've looked at, as a model of fidelity and repentance:

> "I had a very great devotion to the glorious Magdalene, and very frequently used to think of her conversion — especially when I went to Communion. As I knew for certain that our Lord was then within me, I used to place myself at His feet, thinking that my tears would not be despised. I did not know what I was saying; only He did great things for me, in that He was pleased I should shed those tears, seeing that I so soon forgot that impression. I used to recommend myself to that glorious saint, that she might obtain my pardon." (*Life*, 9:2)

The story of Mary Magdalene's contemplative years in the wilderness and her association with the quiet, listening Mary (in contrast to the busy Martha) also appealed to Teresa, unsurprisingly:

> "Let us, then, pray Him always to show His mercy upon us, with a submissive spirit, yet trusting in the goodness of God. And now

> that the soul is permitted to sit at the feet of Christ, let it contrive not to quit its place, but keep it anyhow. Let it follow the example of the Magdalene; and when it shall be strong enough, God will lead it into the wilderness." (*Life*, 21:9)

Asceticism, an important part of Teresa's spirituality (although never to extremes, she firmly taught), was understood by her and others in this period as a means of penance for one's own sins, as well as the sins of others. Here, again, Mary Magdalene was a model:

> "Indeed the body suffers much while alive, for whatever work it does, the soul has energy for far greater tasks and goads it on to more, for all it can perform appears as nothing. This must be the reason of the severe penances performed by many of the saints, especially the glorious Magdalene, who had always spent her life in luxury. This caused the zeal felt by our Father Elias for the honor of God, and the desires of St. Dominic and St. Francis to draw souls to praise the Almighty. I assure you that, forgetful of themselves, they must have passed through no small trials." (*Interior Castle*, 4:16)

Teresa, like many other women, saw in Mary Magdalene a model for faithful discipleship through difficulty, an ideal penitent, and an inspiring contemplative.

### Practical Advice

During this same era, another kind of Catholic reformer was working in another part of Europe. St. Francis de Sales — a gifted writer, preacher, and spiritual director — was the bishop of Geneva, although throughout most of his career, because of the

Calvinist control of that city, he could not openly lead his flock. He wrote, unusually for this period, specifically for the laity, very aware of the particular challenges of living in the world.

His *Introduction to the Devout Life* is a lovely, practical, and charming classic, and it is still indispensable. His letters of spiritual direction, many of them written to his close friend and fellow reformer St. Jane Frances de Chantal, are carefully crafted to answer the specific needs of their recipients. In one of his letters of spiritual direction, written to one Rose Bourgeois, an abbess who, much like Teresa of Ávila, was attempting to reform her own life and that of her convent in a way more faithful to the demands of the Gospel, Francis draws on the image of the contemplative Magdalene in a lovely way:

> **"Dear daughter, what a good way of praying, and what a fine way of staying in God's presence: doing what He wants and accepting what pleases Him! It seems to me that Mary Magdalene was a statue in her niche when, without saying a word, without moving, and perhaps even without looking at Him, she sat at our Lord's feet and listened to what He was saying. When He spoke, she listened; whenever He paused, she stopped listening; but always, she was right there."** (*Letters of Spiritual Direction*, by Francis de Sales and Jane de Chantal [Paulist Press, 1988], p. 152)

### Silent Witness

Mary Magdalene's place in medieval and early modern Catholic spirituality was firm and clear. Her example encouraged Christians to see their own sins clearly and honestly, and hopefully approach the Lord for forgiveness. Her faithfulness to Jesus, an important part of the Passion narratives in the Gospels, was an accessible expression of fidelity. Her identity as a contemplative, fueled by the legend of her time in the wilderness, as well as her identification with Mary, sister of Martha, provided a model for women who sought to pursue a life of deep prayer, singularly devoted to Christ.

But we can see what's been lost, too. In the enthusiasm for repentance, the attraction of the legendary material, we have lost sight of Mary Magdalene, "Apostle to the Apostles." The East certainly kept that aspect of her identity, so firmly attested to in the Gospels and so rich with possibility, and so alive. But in the extraordinary penitential spirit of the West, it was barely spoken of any longer. We can see this, not only in the spiritual uses of Mary Magdalene, but also in the way she has been presented in art.

### Questions for Reflection

1. In what ways did these medieval spiritual writers find Mary Magdalene inspiring?
2. How did they respond to her identity as "Apostle to the Apostles," within the context of their times?
3. Does the image of Mary Magdalene inspire you in similar ways?

# Eleven

# THE MAGDALENE IN ART

*The Da Vinci Code* may be popular, but that doesn't mean that it's right. In fact, Dan Brown's novel is more wrong than right about almost every subject he touches on, from religion to history to the geography of Paris.

Brown's even wrong — very wrong — about art. No, not simply about the details and interpretation of Leonardo's work, but more importantly, Brown is wrong in the *approach* he encourages in looking at art, which, of course, is all about hidden codes and secret information, all embedded in the works — works by Leonardo, Grand Master of the Priory of Sion, an organization which never existed. But we're getting beyond ourselves here. Back to the art.

Art certainly does reach deeper and wider than strokes on a canvas. That is why art endures. But the meaning of art — any art — is gleaned, not by cracking codes, but by contemplating the work, considering its context, learning a bit about the symbolism possibly included in the piece, and contemplating yet again.

Not surprisingly, Mary Magdalene has been a popular subject for artists through the ages. During the heyday of penitential awareness and practice, she was omnipresent in works large and small, drying the feet of Jesus with her hair, praying in the desert, and bringing, sorrowfully, the body of Jesus down from the cross. But even in the early Modern period — the seventeenth and eighteenth centuries — when more art was being commissioned by non-religious institutions and individual wealthy patrons, the Magdalene remained an appealing subject. She was still penitent, but far more eroticized and broadly symbolic, not so much of an individual's repentance before God, but of the enduring tension between spirit and flesh.

### From 'Myrrh-bearer' to Hermit

The earliest artistic depiction of Mary Magdalene we have is a wall painting, probably from an ancient baptistery, dating from the third century in Syria. The scene shows the women approaching the tomb, described in each of the Gospels as including Mary Magdalene. For the first few centuries of Christianity's existence, this was the usual — if not the only — depiction of Mary, and it was a very popular scene.

In the early Middle Ages, as more churches were being constructed, and as more art was produced to decorate them and catechize the faithful, a second depiction of Mary became standard: Mary Magdalene at the foot of the cross, always mourning, sometimes even supporting the Virgin Mary in her own quiet grief.

(Incidentally, the question of the Virgin's grief was controversial. Early Church Fathers had condemned excessive weeping and mourning as unseemly for Christians who have faith in the Resurrection. St. Ambrose argued in the fourth century specifically that the Virgin could not have mourned because she knew Jesus would rise from the dead [Haskins, p. 201].)

Mary Magdalene also gained a place in post-Crucifixion scenes, as Jesus' body is taken from the cross and buried. In the Middle Ages, she was often shown in the process of anointing or cleaning, sometimes even with her hair, caring for Jesus' feet, a clear evocation of the now-common association of Mary Magdalene with the repentant woman in Luke 7, as well as with Mary of Bethany.

Mary Magdalene can be identified in art by the presence of a jar, either in her hand, or nearby on the ground. The jar recalls her role in preparing Jesus' body for burial and the anointing at Bethany.

As those associations became embedded in popular piety, the figure of the penitent Magdalene evolved into a powerful and common figure in art. Depictions of the scene in Luke 7 were included in various series painted on Mary Magdalene's life. One such series, a fresco by Giovanni da Milano in a chapel in Florence, visually conflates Luke's stories by showing Mary cleansing Jesus' feet and, at the same time, seven black demons flying out of the roof of the house (Haskins, p. 195).

*The Golden Legend* standardized the now-enduring story in the West of Mary Magdalene in Provence. There was some art created that dramatized the boat ride of Mary Magdalene, Martha, and Lazarus across the sea from the Holy Land. But what inspired artists and those who commissioned them more than anything else from this period was Mary's decades of contemplation and penance in the caves of Ste-Baume.

Because Mary functioned as a figure of hope and inspiration to Christians highly aware of their own sinfulness, this image had a great deal of power. She was always portrayed kneeling, hands folded in prayer, sometimes with one or more of the symbols associated with her nearby.

> Aside from the jar, depictions of the penitent Magdalene often included a skull, as a symbol of earthly life and its ultimate end, and an open book, evoking contemplation and prayer.

From very early on in the Middle Ages, Mary Magdalene was often depicted as nude in these portraits of her eremitical (hermit) life. The reason, initially at least, had nothing to do with eroticism. In medieval art, nudity was a symbol of purity, of single-minded focus on God, and of the innocence of the Garden of Eden. If you look, for example, at portrayals of St. Jerome, who also spent time in the wilderness, translating the Bible into Latin in caves outside Jerusalem, his emaciated body is often very scantily clad as well.

It's not supposed to stimulate us, except spiritually. It's a sign that the person focused on God is, in some sense, separate from the world and its concerns, and is being brought back to the original state of Adam and Eve through intimacy with God.

In these early medieval days, Mary Magdalene's body was usually covered with her long tresses — again, we see the connection to the woman of Luke 7. There's also a connection with other saintly legends in which women, their innocence and virginity threatened, suddenly grow long locks of hair to cover their bodies. Her hair, too, was probably intended to evoke the formerly sexually profligate life of the legendary Magdalene.

However, as time went on, artistic values shifted. During the Renaissance, the cultural center of energy was not God, but the human person and the human figure. While in previous eras the human figure had functioned as a symbol pointing to something more, Renaissance artists — and later Baroque-period artists — had a keen interest in the human figure for its own sake, and the art featuring Mary Magdalene reflected this. In short, her hair covered less and less.

She was still kneeling (although in later pieces, she was often lying down), and she still might have had her hands folded, but her hair had been moved aside, and most of the time her breasts were exposed, which again, was not unusual in this period, nor was it necessarily an erotic image. But gradually, spiritual content diminished, as Mary's hair covered less and less, and her pose served to accent the female figure rather than evoke anything like penance. As Susan Haskins writes of the late sixteenth and seventeenth centuries: "In the hands of lesser artists . . . the saint became little more than a beautiful woman, an idealized feminine body rather than a repentant sinner, similar to the many paintings of courtesans of the period, her attributes — the jar or skull — often being the only means by which she might be distinguished. She became, to use Mario Praz's words, the 'great amorous penitent' or 'Venus in sackcloth' " (Haskins, p. 257).

Some portrayals of Mary Magdalene in the wilderness clothed her in animal hair, similar to portraits of St. Jerome, St. Anthony, or St. John the Baptist, or even hair that had miraculously grown all over her body. *The Elevation of the Magdalene*, a sixteenth-century work by Peter Strub the Younger, depicts the part of the legend that describes Mary being lifted to heaven during the hours of prayer. She is sheathed in fur — except at her knees, where it has been worn bare by her prayer.

Some depictions of Mary Magdalene during this period used her as a symbol of classically defined traits, particularly *vanitas, luxuria*, and *melancholia* — Vanity, Luxury, and Melancholy. These works usually centered on the theme of the conversion of Mary Magdalene, as she contemplates, often in a mirror, the life she is thinking of leaving (and its transience — hence, Melancholy) — a concept rooted in the legends about Mary being a wealthy, perhaps promiscuous woman before she met Christ.

(The association of Mary Magdalene with these concepts was also common in medieval preaching, as preachers sought to discourage women from dressing and adorning themselves ostentatiously.)

We know we have traveled a very far distance from the myrrhbearers of the third century when we find out that by the eighteenth century it was very popular for wealthy women to have themselves portrayed in paintings as the Magdalene, in fetching, barely clothed, and barely penitent poses.

The way to that point in history is complex, the result of a dynamic of artistic and spiritual values, in the context of a culture that, while still outwardly very religious, was loosening itself from a religious foundation, rapidly, yet subtly establishing a secular realm in which artists would create, in response not as much to religious sensibilities as to the desires of wealthy patrons. Religious art was still being created, and Mary Magdalene figured in some of it, certainly. But her function, even in some of this religious art, had shifted:

> The medieval Magdalene was a (former) sinner, but that aspect of her legend was only important insofar as through it sinful people were brought to salvation. Now, however, she was interesting precisely as an exciting, seductively beautiful sinner. What people wanted was no longer the patron and advocate, but the loving and penitent sinner.... Her true task was no longer that of the advocate; she had become a symbol reflecting the fragility of life and the world. (*Mary Magdalene: The Image of a Woman Through the Centuries*, by Ingrid Maisch [Liturgical Press, 1998], p. 66)

Times had changed. Art, as it always does, reflected that change. Some contemporary writers would have us believe that the figure of Mary Magdalene as a disheveled, half-nude, eroticized former prostitute is the product of a Christian plot to minimize her, to put her in a box so that the true nature of her role would be hidden. As we can see, this is not exactly the way it happened. While it is true that in the West the figure of the Penitent Magdalene came to dominate, no one ever stopped creating art depicting her role as "Myrrh-bearer" and witness to the Resurrection. The shift to Mary as Wanton Woman, it should be clear, had nothing to do with the Church, and everything to do with contemporary fashion — in fact, during the Counter-Reformation period, Church officials sometimes attempted to regulate the content of religiously themed art, discouraging, in the case of Mary Magdalene, the use of nudity and images from *The Golden Legend*.

Mary's role as a model of penitence may have distracted Christians from her post-Resurrection role, which was highlighted in the Gospels. But perhaps, in the broader sense, it's all of a piece. After all, what is the message of the Resurrection? That there is life after death. In a way, the figure of Mary as forgiven, contemplating the mercy of God, is a powerful embodiment — or dare we say, witness — of that very fact.

**Here are other popular depictions of Mary Magdalene:**

- **Placing her with the Virgin and the infant Jesus.**
- ***Noli Me Tangere:*** **the dramatization of John 20:17, usually with Mary reaching out and Jesus holding his hand out to discourage her, and perhaps with Jesus raising his other hand toward the heavens.**
- **Grouping her with other saints like St. Clare, St. Catherine of Siena, or St. Dominic.**
- **Preaching, smashing pagan idols, and even baptizing: these are particularly numerous in France, not surprisingly.**
- **Receiving her last Communion from St. Maximin.**

## On Stage

Medieval Christians learned about their faith, not only through preaching and art, but also through drama.

Liturgy was intrinsically dramatic, of course, but aside from that, dramatic dialogues found their way into Christian liturgies in the early Middle Ages. Important feast days often included, either before or after, some dramatized presentation related to the celebration. For example, as Susan Haskins notes, in the tenth century, in some cathedrals and monasteries, a dialogue was presented during Easter Matins that featured a lament from Mary Magdalene.

As time went on, the presentations grew more elaborate, incorporating scenes, for example, of Mary negotiating for her ointments or collapsing at the tomb. The hymn *Victimae Paschali Laudes*, which was used in the Easter liturgy for centuries, originated as a part of one of these dramatic presentations:

> "Tell us, Mary,
> What did you see on the way?
> I saw the sepulcher of the living Christ,
> And I saw the glory of the Resurrected one:
> The Angelic witnesses,
> The winding cloth, and His garments."
>
> (*Victimae Paschali Laudes*, eleventh century)

Throughout the medieval period, drama floated free of the liturgy and took root in European life as mystery plays, the fruit of which we see even today in the form of Passion plays. Mystery plays were often quite elaborate affairs, sometimes traveling shows, and at other times annual productions of a particular community. Their subjects could be as broad as the entire history of salvation or as specific as the life of a particular saint.

Mary Magdalene would obviously be a popular subject, and indeed she was. Her pre-conversion life — inspired by the legend, but certainly not limited by it — provided an opportunity to dramatize a life of luxury and decadence, personifying, as she often did in art and preaching of the period, *luxuria* and *vanitas*, at once both titillating and cautionary.

One of the more intensely studied examples of this genre is the Digby *Mary Magdalene*, written in England some time in the late fifteenth century. It calls for over fifty speaking parts and contains twenty-one hundred lines. The play covers Mary's life from before her conversion to her death, consistent with the legend, after her long years of contemplation in the cave in Provence. The play's directions call for nineteen different settings, and a great deal of elaborate stage machinery, including a moving ship, clouds for descending and ascending, and the means for the devil, who is featured in the play as he attempts to keep Mary Magdalene in his grasp, to descend into hell. The play packs much of the legendary material we have discussed, placing special emphasis on Jesus' sending of Mary Magdalene as a "holy apostylesse" to France, and dramatizing her performing miracles and even speaking in tongues.

## Life Imitates Art

In another time, another place, Christians lived in an art-saturated culture, which was dynamic and creative. Christian spirituality was nurtured, not just on Sundays, and not just in words, but in images that peeked out at Christians from the facades of their churches — as well as from the interiors — and from the illuminations in their prayer books, and in their entertainment as well.

Mary Magdalene, with a life story that had evolved into one that embodied the temptations, grief, and hope of every Christian, was a naturally popular subject for artistic expression during these centuries, not because Church officials were determined to impose a certain image of her, but because the image that had taken hold in the popular mind was appealing, interesting, and hopeful.

### Questions for Reflection

1. What are the primary symbols that characterize Mary Magdalene in art?
2. How did the image of Mary Magdalene in art change over the years?
3. What is the image of Mary Magdalene in the popular mind today?

# Twelve

# REDISCOVERY

So, what has happened to Mary Magdalene?
Where did she go?

Mary's role in the spiritual lives of ordinary Christians in the West has inarguably faded to near-invisibility, a startling contrast to her dominance in the medieval period. But then, so have most saints. The collapse of Catholic culture and the deemphasis on devotion to saints in the post-Vatican II Church has taken its obvious toll on the Catholic devotion to saints in general, pushing these holy men and women to the fringes of Catholic public and private spirituality. Mary Magdalene is just one of too many "casualties" to count.

But she's not totally forgotten, of course. There's an entire industry that has sprung up around her name over the past decade or so — books, workshops, and speakers who have seized on Mary Magdalene as a symbol, but not of penitence, of hope in Christ, or of "Apostle to the Apostles," as she was understood by traditional Christianity. No, for these contemporary interpreters, she is the "Goddess in the Gospels," the "Beloved Spouse" of Jesus, the Holy Grail, or the real founder of Christianity. Some of these uses of the Magdalene are interesting and genuinely provocative. Others are just silly, and in the end insulting to what we know of the real Mary Magdalene.

## 'Magdalene Christianity'

The history of early Christianity is not without ambiguity. While the textual evidence we have from those first three centuries is actually surprisingly hefty — given the fact that we are talking about a small, persecuted movement a millennium and a half ago

— these same texts do not leave us with all of our questions answered.

There was a clear line of development from Jesus to the apostles and on through Paul and the establishment of Christian communities, those groups that held beliefs about Jesus, his ministry, and the purpose of the Church that we would call orthodox: those that self-consciously molded themselves according to what Jesus had taught, as preserved and passed on by the apostles.

But as any historian can tell you, this community was not static. It did not possess full and complete self-understanding from the beginning. From that beginning, there were different interpretations of Jesus, his call, and what that meant for those who followed him, and orthodox Christianity continued to define itself by reflecting on the words of Jesus in that context. The dynamic is something we all experience: sometimes we vaguely understand something, but it is only in dialogue, or in even dispute, with someone else, that we really do grasp the idea. That dialogue is clarifying.

So it was with the early Christians — and it happened almost right away, as they faced the question of what do about Gentiles, or non-Jews, who wanted to become Christian. Would they have to become Jewish as well? Would they have to be circumcised and adhere to the Law? The process of working that out clarified some important elements of Jesus' teaching that were not intuitively obvious to those first, all-Jewish believers.

However, those who "lost" — those who did, indeed, believe that Jesus' disciples should also follow Jewish law — did not go away. The "Judaizers" — referred to by Paul, particularly in his letter to the Galatians — continued their own teaching, and did so, we think, up through the second century.

Now, does the existence of this group tell us that there were "many Christianities," all equally valid? Not really. It tells us that there were, indeed, different interpretations of Jesus' identity and mission, but it does not follow that this interpretation of Jesus is correct.

Now, some would say that there is no such thing as a more or less correct interpretation of Jesus. However, I sincerely doubt that those who would argue that position would hold fast to it, say, when looking at the ideas of those who claim to be Christian and at the same time are white supremacists. Is that "interpretation" of Jesus valid, and is it simply an "alternative Christianity" on par with the orthodox Christian teaching? No. Obviously, there are lines to be drawn, and while they are sometimes fuzzy, the essential ones are those that take the apostolic witness to the totality of Jesus' presence, teaching, passion, and resurrection seriously and humbly.

This is the context in which we have to see the current conversation about a possible "Magdalene Christianity." The vision is essentially this: that in some early Christian communities, Mary Magdalene was recognized as a leader on par with the apostles — and perhaps even superior to them — and in those communities, a radically egalitarian vision of life was pursued.

There are different forms of this story, to be sure. Some suggest a full-blown competition between separate sects, one led by Mary Magdalene, the other by Peter. Others are more nuanced, describing a conflict between early Christian factions based not so much on gender issues but instead on disagreements between those who looked to charismatic qualities (that is, the gifts of the Holy Spirit) as a basis of leadership and those rooted more in institutional concerns, with Mary Magdalene as the representative of the former.

The canonical Gospels are read by these writers for hints of conflict and political jockeying. Other writings, some orthodox Christian, others Gnostic or expressive of other streams of thought, are also studied closely for the same clues. We don't have time to take on all of the various theories floating around in academia and popular culture, but what is most important is that we come to some understanding of how to interpret these theories in general.

The first and most fundamental point is to read beyond the headlines, beyond the book-jacket blurbs, and even beyond the text on the page. Most of the time, breathless interpretations of a newly discovered role for Mary Magdalene in early Christianity are not nearly as clear-cut as their proponents would have you believe. They are often dependent on, for example, highly idiosyncratic text dating — placing, for instance, the *Gospel of Mary* a hundred years earlier than most scholars would. They are also dependent on interpretations of texts, whether they are canonical Scripture or extra-biblical material, which are shaped by expectations, and hence are not objective. We saw an example of this in Chapter 3 on Gnostic writings, when we learned that some scholars are beginning to question the widespread and automatic association of every "Mary" in the Gnostic writings with Mary Magdalene, especially those that came from a Syrian milieu, in which the Virgin Mary was highly venerated.

The other point, which must be emphasized again and again, is that while there were certainly disputes within early Christianity regarding leadership — one need only read the epistles of Paul to see this clearly — there is really no firm evidence that there was any distinctive circle of Christians gathered around the figure of Mary Magdalene. While it is true that even the legendary material from both East and West reflects a respect for her preaching, does this actually reflect an ancient memory of a Christian branch in which Mary Magdalene was a leader and foundress? Most scholars, even those with no particular interest in the claims of orthodox Christianity, would say no.

The ultimate irony is that the proponents of a "Magdalene Christianity" base their claims on inconsistent treatment of, on the one hand, the canonical Gospels and, on the other hand, their own chosen texts.

Quite simply, it's this: These writers would, to a person, claim that the canonical Gospels cannot be read on face value, that they do not tell us anything much about the events they claim to describe, but that they *do* tell us everything about the communities that produced them. So, for example, the Resurrection narratives do not tell us that Jesus rose from the dead — as they seem to rather plainly state — but instead tell us that Peter associated himself with this story in order to claim leadership in the post-Jesus Christian movement. (Why in the world he would want to do this is, of course, never addressed.)

However, when proponents of the Mary-Magdalene-as-Christian-Leader school turn to the Gnostic writings, they bring a completely different set of expectations. Now, it seems, we have history clearly and directly written. If it says the apostles were jealous of Mary Magdalene's role in Jesus' life, then the apostles *were* jealous. The canonical Gospels, written decades after the events described, apparently tell us little or nothing about those events and only about the agenda of the community telling the story, while the Gnostic writings, composed a century or more after the events described, tell us the truth about the events, rather than anything about the agenda of the community telling the story.

Some of this newer scholarship is worth reading, but much of it is not. But whatever you do, confront this material with your own copy of the Scriptures and whatever other texts at hand, as well as your own critical sense, watching out for unwarranted assumptions. Search the Internet for the writings of critics of these scholars, and make your own judgment.

As ambiguous as some of the history of early Christianity may be, there really are not deep dark secrets threatening to shake the foundations. They used to call it Gnosticism, and perhaps they still should, for that's exactly what's being replayed here most of the time, just in more modern clothes.

### Goddess and Grail

At least "Magdalene Christianity" draws on something real — the existence of various interpretations of Jesus that existed during the first four centuries. Some of the more popular thinking about Mary Magdalene over the past ten years cannot even claim that: namely, the idea that Mary Magdalene was married to Jesus, bore his child, and that her role as "Bride" is really central to Christianity, as Jesus intended it.

*The Da Vinci Code*, of course, fictionalizes this theory, which is actually heady fiction all by itself. The writer upon whom Brown depends for many of his ideas, and who has single-handedly popularized this notion, is Margaret Starbird.

Starbird's work weaves together Gnostic writings, medieval legends, code-obsessed readings of art and artifacts, as well as some of the more recent Templar-based conspiracy theories related to Mary Magdalene into books that are invariably misplaced in bookstores in the "Nonfiction" section.

What we have in Starbird's work is, basically, a net. She catches everything related to Mary Magdalene. She even, interestingly enough, accepts St. Gregory the Great's conflation of the Marys. And then, she concocts a stew out of it, shaping the "evidence" to support her own theories:

> The real Mary Magdalen, although later called prostitute by the church, was never scorned by Jesus in the Gospels. She was the love of his life. As in the fairy tales, the handsome prince has been seeking her for two thousand years, trying to restore her to her rightful place at his side. (*The Woman with the Alabaster Jar: Mary Magdalene and the Holy Grail* [Bear & Company, 1993], pp. 176-177)

This Mary is, according to Starbird, a goddess, the embodiment of the sacred feminine. This truth has been buried by orthodox Christianity for years, she says, but now can be revealed and discerned through unorthodox means. One of Starbird's techniques is the use of gematria, or de-coding the Greek text of the New Testament according to numerological principles. She works from the traditional numerical values given to Greek letters, and from that she discerns a code of meaning which she claims reveals that those who wrote the Gospels believed and were secretly communicating that Mary Magdalene was a goddess, and the beloved of Jesus:

> "The evidence that Mary Magdalene and Jesus together provided the model for the 'hieros gamos' (Sacred Marriage) in Christianity is found in the Gospels themselves. The numbers coded by gematria in her name indicate that Mary Magdalene was the 'Goddess' among early Christians. They understood the 'numbers theology' of the Hellenistic world, numbers coded in the New Testament that were based on the ancient canon of sacred geometry derived by the Pythagoreans centuries before.
>
> "The Greek epithet 'h Magdalhnh' bears the number 153, a profoundly important value used among mathematicians to designate the Vesica Piscis — the ()-shape identified with the 'sacred Feminine' in the ancient world. This symbol, the 'vulva,' has obvious attributes of feminine regeneration and the 'doorway' or 'portal' of life — the 'sacred cauldron of creativity.' It was a very ancient ancient [sic], even archetypal symbol for the Goddess. It was called the 'holy of holies' and the 'inner sanctum.' Almonds were sacred to Venus. The symbol abounds in cave art of ancient peoples discovered in shrines where the fertility of the earth and the female was honored. It was no accident that the epithet of Mary Magdalene bore the number that to the educated of the time identified her as the 'Goddess in the Gospels.'"
>
> (Margaret Starbird, at www.magdalene.org)

One can look at this from a number of different perspectives, but we will begin and end with logic. If the writers of the New Testament believed this — that Jesus and Mary Magdalene were espoused and that Mary was a goddess — why couldn't they just say so? There would have been no recriminations coming their way for doing so. If that was the truth about what Christianity was, it could have easily been openly preached in the Roman Empire of the first century. In fact, to do so would have brought much less pain and suffering to those early Christians. One can't help but wonder why they would choose to cover the truth of what they supposedly believed with lies that got them imprisoned and executed. That would be strange, indeed, and would require a whole other set of codes to understand.

## Reaching for the Stars

In the third through the fifth centuries, Gnostics used the characters of Jesus and Mary Magdalene as just that — characters in a story they were trying to tell about their own mythologies and worldview. The names were there, but little else from the first-century sources that are the most reliable historical guides to the identities, words, and actions of the early Christians. Gnostics felt free to ignore the historical record and invent their own vision of the past that supported their own ideology.

Much of the same thing is happening today. There are plenty of books being published on Mary Magdalene, plenty of words being spoken on her behalf, in her voice. But most of them are simply exercises in imaginative speculation, writings that either explicitly reject the historical texts of the first century or reinterpret them in extreme, fantastical ways, in order to suit an agenda. Many of these writers will try to tell us that it is very important for us to "listen to" Mary Magdalene, that she has a great deal to say to us that is vital and life-changing.

We can't help but agree. We also would prefer to listen to *her* — as she speaks in the Gospels — not through the imagination of her modern interpreters, with their own agendas and blind spots.

## Questions for Reflection

1. Why do you think some contemporary writers use Mary Magdalene in the way that they do?

2. What similarities do you see between this kind of thinking and ancient Gnostic thinking?

3. Why do you think some modern commentators prefer to focus on a mythical or imaginary Mary Magdalene, rather than the Mary of the Gospels?

# EPILOGUE

As we come to the end of our journey, we can look back on countless legends, stories, and speculations regarding Mary Magdalene. She has stood as a symbol of devotion, fidelity, repentance, and gratitude to millions of Christians throughout history.

But what, in the end, can we say about *who* Mary Magdalene really was? What did happen to her after the Ascension of Jesus?

There is no way, given the evidence that we have at hand right now, to know the answer with absolute certainty. Nonetheless, it is possible — in considering the various historically rooted legends of antiquity, the travels of the purported relics of Mary Magdalene, and the devotion to her in various parts of the world — to consider some serious possibilities.

> Given the strong Eastern tradition, which is quite ancient, it is highly probable that Mary Magdalene indeed accompanied John and the Virgin Mary to Ephesus after the Ascension, where she eventually died and was buried. Her relics were transferred to Constantinople in the ninth century, from where some of them eventually made their way to southern France. It is possible to imagine that the arrival of the relics in this area inspired an evangelizing fervor and led to conversions to Christianity, which is depicted, in an imaginative way, in the legends about Mary Magdalene preaching, converting, and baptizing in this area.

Ancient Christian legends come to us through the centuries, shrouded in mystery, even as they are, still rooted in the Gospels. Ultimately, even in their eccentric paths, they all point to Christ. Through the mists of time, it just might be possible to discern — underlying and inspiring the fantastic — some fascinating possible truths about what really happened to Mary Magdalene, "Apostle to the Apostles," whose presence, even in the form of her relics, worked to spread the Good News of salvation through Jesus the Son of God.

## Whither the Magdalene?

I hope reading this book has been educational for you. Writing it certainly has been for me. Again and again I have been forced to reflect on the powerful, positive impact that the figure of Mary Magdalene once had on Christianity, and frankly, to mourn its loss.

What modern critics say about the traditional *cultus* of Mary Magdalene is just not true. They seek to redeem her, claiming that traditional Christianity reviled her as a prostitute. As we've seen, that is just not so. While Mary Magdalene's legendary pre-conversion life was, indeed, used to correct the perceived sins of women, and later became an object of titillation rather than inspiration, it should be quite clear by now that Mary Magdalene was never reviled in traditional Christianity, never demeaned, and never dismissed.

She was the most popular saint of the Middle Ages. She was beloved, revered, and looked to as living proof of the great mercy of God. And once again, we are forced to ask: What happened?

The sad irony is that in getting the Mary Magdalene story right, in correcting St. Gregory the Great's "mistake," a thousand years of rationale for honoring Mary Magdalene in the West was, with a stroke, wiped out. This image had come to dominate thinking about her to such an extent that Western Christians had nothing left in terms of devotional practices or spiritual writing to help them keep a place for Mary Magdalene.

It is a story that brings us to that hard place in Christian tradition, of discerning between fact and legend, and trying to make sense of the latter. For, the skeptic might ask, why criticize Starbird and her ilk? Doesn't her work perform the same function as those medieval legends?

Not exactly. And note, we are not advocating the retrieval of the legendary material as the center of Magdalene devotion. Not by any means. However, traditional Christian elaboration on the Mary Magdalene story, even as it embroidered a complex tapestry that seems far from the Gospels, was, in fact, not so far from the Gospels after all. In these legends, Mary Magdalene is devoted to the Jesus, not of her own making, but the Jesus of the Gospels. The themes that course through the legends are Gospel themes: repentance, new life, and discipleship. No, these legends should not be the center of our devotion to Mary Magdalene, for we are better served by sticking to what the Gospels tell us. But the truth is, these legends do not take us away from the Gospels as do these modern interpreters. The legends reinforce the Gospels, in strange, delightful, and engaging ways.

However, I want to end this book with a plea for Christians of the West to once again pay serious attention to Mary Magdalene, as a great saint and model for us all, male and female. We need not worry about Provence or Ephesus to do so, but simply return to the Gospels, and to the truth about Mary Magdalene preserved there, and so powerfully preserved in the Christian Churches of the East.

We live in a world in which Christians are warned to be silent. To keep our beliefs to ourselves. To keep quiet about the astonishing love of God and his power to change lives, bringing light into darkness, turning sorrow into joy.

Mary Magdalene stands in the garden, a rebuke to that warning. She, grateful for what Jesus had done for her, could not leave his side, even in danger. She, having seen the Lord, could not be silent, even knowing how incredible her story sounded and how disreputable a witness she might be. She loved, she anointed, she saw, and she heard. When asked what she had seen — *Dic nobis?* — she spoke. Fearlessly, joyfully, heedless of the consequences.

*St. Mary Magdalene, pray for us.*

# FOR FURTHER READING

The literature on St. Mary Magdalene is considerable, but it presents two problems. First, there is a great deal of interesting scholarly work that has been published, but much of it is only in academic journals or not yet available in English. Second, much of the literature that is accessible to the non-academic reader is politically charged and ideologically driven.

Some of the works below do, indeed, bear an agenda, some more lightly than others. However, much of this information about the historical development of the *cultus* of Mary Magdalene is not available in any other printed sources.

- *Mary Magdalene: Myth and Metaphor*, by Susan Haskins (Berkley, 1997). This is a lengthy, detailed work that explores the image of the saint from the earliest centuries of Christianity through the modern period. It includes not only liturgy, prayer, and devotional art but also institutions inspired by Mary Magdalene and secular reflections.
- *The Making of the Magdalen: Preaching and Popular Devotion in the Later Middle Ages*, by Katherine Ludwig Jansen (Princeton University Press, 2000). This is not only a beautiful, objective examination of the wealth of devotion poured out to Mary Magdalene during this period, but it also includes useful information on the saint's life and early history.
- *Mary Magdalene: The Image of a Woman Through the Centuries*, by Ingrid Maisch (Liturgical Press, 1998). This is a look at the interpretations of Mary Magdalene, with a focus on German-speaking cultures, but inclusive of early Christianity as well.

- *The Life of St. Mary Magdalene and of Her Sister St. Martha*, by Rabanus Maurus, translated and annotated by David Mycoff (Cistercian Publications, 1989). This invaluable little volume by Rabanus Maurus (784?-856), archbishop of Mainz, offers a direct look at the nature of medieval devotion to Mary Magdalene.
- *Women in the Ministry of Jesus*, by Ben Witherington III (Cambridge University Press, 1984). Scripture scholar Witherington's objective work is helpful for putting the Mary Magdalene of the Gospels in context.
- *Hidden Gospels: How the Search for Jesus Lost Its Way*, by Philip Jenkins (Oxford University Press, 2001). This is an important source for clarifying issues related to the Gnostic writings many use to interpret Mary Magdalene today.

# MARY MAGDALENE IN THE GOSPELS

*The following are the Gospel passages that relate to Mary Magdalene, directly or indirectly. The Catholic edition of the Revised Standard Version of the Bible is the translation used.*

*This passage is the only mention of Mary Magdalene outside of the Passion and Resurrection narratives.*

### Luke 8:1-3

Soon afterward he went on through cities and villages, preaching and bringing the good news of the kingdom of God. And the twelve were with him, and also some women who had been healed of evil spirits and infirmities: Mary, called Magdalene, from whom seven demons had gone out, and Joanna, the wife of Chuza, Herod's steward, and Susanna, and many others, who provided for them out of their means.

*Mary Magdalene is mentioned, in all of the Gospels, as being present at the death of Jesus and the deposition of his body. (Luke does not mention her name because her identity as one of the women from Galilee would be understood.)*

### Matthew 27:55-61

There were also many women there, looking on from afar, who had followed Jesus from Galilee, ministering to him; among whom were Mary Magdalene, and Mary the mother of James and Joseph, and the mother of the sons of Zebedee.

When it was evening, there came a rich man from Arimathea, named Joseph, who also was a disciple of Jesus. He went to Pilate and asked for the body of Jesus. Then Pilate ordered it to be given to him. And Joseph took the body, and wrapped it in a clean linen shroud, and laid it in his own new tomb, which he had hewn in the rock; and he rolled a great stone to the door of the tomb, and departed. Mary Magdalene and the other Mary were there, sitting opposite the sepulchre.

### Mark 15:40-47

There were also women looking on from afar, among whom were Mary Magdalene, and Mary the mother of James the younger and of Joses, and Salome, who, when he was in Galilee, followed him, and ministered to him; and also many other women who came up with him to Jerusalem.

And when evening had come, since it was the day of Preparation, that is, the day before the sabbath, Joseph of Arimathea, a respected member of the council, who was also himself looking for the kingdom of God, took courage and went to Pilate, and asked for the body of Jesus. And Pilate wondered if he were already dead; and summoning the centurion, he asked him whether he was already dead. And when he learned from the centurion that he was dead, he granted the body to Joseph. And he bought a linen shroud, and taking him down, wrapped him in the linen shroud, and laid him in a tomb which had been hewn out of the rock; and he rolled a stone against the door of the tomb. Mary Magdalene and Mary the mother of Joses saw where he was laid.

### Luke 23:49-56

And all his acquaintances and the women who had followed him from Galilee stood at a distance and saw these things.

Now there was a man named Joseph from the Jewish town of Arimathea. He was a member of the council, a good and righteous man, who had not consented to their purpose and deed, and he was looking for the kingdom of God. This man went to Pilate and asked for the body of Jesus. Then he took it down and wrapped it in a linen shroud, and laid him in a rock-hewn tomb, where no one had ever yet been laid. It was the day of Preparation, and the sabbath was beginning. The women who had come with him from Galilee followed, and saw the tomb, and how his body was laid; then they returned, and prepared spices and ointments.

On the sabbath they rested according to the commandment.

### John 19:25

But standing by the cross of Jesus were his mother, and his mother's sister, Mary the wife of Clopas, and Mary Magdalene.

*All four Gospels agree that Mary Magdalene was among the first witnesses of the empty tomb. (John highlights her role, placing her at the tomb, encountering the risen Jesus alone.)*

### Matthew 28:1-10

Now after the sabbath, toward the dawn of the first day of the week, Mary Magdalene and the other Mary went to see the sepulchre. And behold, there was a great earthquake; for an angel of the Lord descended from heaven and came and rolled back the stone, and sat upon it. His appearance was like lightning, and his raiment white as snow. And for fear of him the guards trembled and became like dead men. But the angel said to the women, "Do not be afraid; for I know that you seek Jesus who was crucified. He is not here; for he has risen, as he said. Come, see the place where he lay. Then go quickly and tell his disciples that he has risen from the dead, and behold, he is going before you to Galilee; there you will see him. Lo, I have told you." So they departed quickly from the tomb with fear and great joy, and ran to tell his disciples. And behold, Jesus met them and said, "Hail!" And they came up and took hold of his feet and worshiped him. Then Jesus said to them, "Do not be afraid; go and tell my brethren to go to Galilee, and there they will see me."

## Mark 16:1-11

And when the sabbath was past, Mary Magdalene, and Mary the mother of James, and Salome, bought spices, so that they might go and anoint him. And very early on the first day of the week they went to the tomb when the sun had risen. And they were saying to one another, "Who will roll away the stone for us from the door of the tomb?" And looking up, they saw that the stone was rolled back; for it was very large. And entering the tomb, they saw a young man sitting on the right side, dressed in a white robe; and they were amazed. And he said to them, "Do not be amazed; you seek Jesus of Nazareth, who was crucified. He has risen, he is not here; see the place where they laid him. But go, tell his disciples and Peter that he is going before you to Galilee; there you will see him, as he told you." And they went out and fled from the tomb; for trembling and astonishment had come upon them; and they said nothing to any one, for they were afraid.

Now when he rose early on the first day of the week, he appeared first to Mary Magdalene, from whom he had cast out seven demons. She went and told those who had been with him, as they mourned and wept. But when they heard that he was alive and had been seen by her, they would not believe it.

## Luke 24:1-11

But on the first day of the week, at early dawn, they went to the tomb, taking the spices which they had prepared. And they found the stone rolled away from the tomb, but when they went in they did not find the body. While they were perplexed about this, behold, two men stood by them in dazzling apparel; and as they were frightened and bowed their faces to the ground, the men said to them, "Why do you seek the living among the dead? He is not here, but has risen. Remember how he told you, while he was still in Galilee, that the Son of man must be delivered into the hands of sinful men, and be crucified, and on the third day rise." And they remembered his words, and returning from the tomb they told all this to the eleven and to all the rest. Now it was Mary Magdalene and Joanna and Mary the mother of James and the other women with them who told this to the apostles; but these words seemed to them an idle tale, and they did not believe them.

### John 20: 1-18

Now on the first day of the week Mary Magdalene came to the tomb early, while it was still dark, and saw that the stone had been taken away from the tomb. So she ran, and went to Simon Peter and the other disciple, the one whom Jesus loved, and said to them, "They have taken the Lord out of the tomb, and we do not know where they have laid him." Peter then came out with the other disciple, and they went toward the tomb. They both ran, but the other disciple outran Peter and reached the tomb first; and stooping to look in, he saw the linen cloths lying there, but he did not go in. Then Simon Peter came, following him, and went into the tomb; he saw the linen cloths lying, and the napkin, which had been on his head, not lying with the linen cloths but rolled up in a place by itself. Then the other disciple, who reached the tomb first, also went in, and he saw and believed; for as yet they did not know the scripture, that he must rise from the dead. Then the disciples went back to their homes.

But Mary stood weeping outside the tomb, and as she wept she stooped to look into the tomb; and she saw two angels in white, sitting where the body of Jesus had lain, one at the head and one at the feet. They said to her, "Woman, why are you weeping?" She said to them, "Because they have taken away my Lord, and I do not know where they have laid him." Saying this, she turned round and saw Jesus standing, but she did not know that it was Jesus. Jesus said to her, "Woman, why are you weeping? Whom do you seek?" Supposing him to be the gardener, she said to him, "Sir, if you have carried him away, tell me where you have laid him, and I will take him away." Jesus said to her, "Mary." She turned and said to him in Hebrew, "Rabboni!" (which means Teacher). Jesus said to her, "Do not hold me, for I have not yet ascended to the Father; but go to my brethren and say to them, I am ascending to my Father and your Father, to my God and your God." Mary Magdalene went and said to the disciples, "I have seen the Lord"; and she told them that he had said these things to her.

*In addition to the above passages that indisputably refer to Mary Magdalene, two other passages have been very important in the Christian tradition's understanding of the saint. The first is the story in Luke that directly precedes the introduction of Mary Magdalene. Because of its proximity, the association of sinfulness with Mary's demonic possession, as well as the anointing motif, evocative of Mary Magdalene, for centuries this woman was identified as Mary Magdalene, and this was the Gospel reading at Mass on her feast day.*

## Luke 7:36-50

One of the Pharisees asked him to eat with him, and he went into the Pharisee's house, and sat at table. And behold, a woman of the city, who was a sinner, when she learned that he was sitting at table in the Pharisee's house, brought an alabaster flask of ointment, and standing behind him at his feet, weeping, she began to wet his feet with her tears, and wiped them with the hair of her head, and kissed his feet, and anointed them with the ointment. Now when the Pharisee who had invited him saw it, he said to himself, "If this man were a prophet, he would have known who and what sort of woman this is who is touching him, for she is a sinner." And Jesus answering said to him, "Simon, I have something to say to you." And he answered, "What is it, Teacher?" "A certain creditor had two debtors; one owed five hundred denarii, and the other fifty. When they could not pay, he forgave them both. Now which of them will love him more?" Simon answered, "The one, I suppose, to whom he forgave more." And he said to him, "You have judged rightly." Then turning toward the woman he said to Simon, "Do you see this woman? I entered your house, you gave me no water for my feet, but she has wet my feet with her tears and wiped them with her hair. You gave me no kiss, but from the time I came in she has not ceased to kiss my feet. You did not anoint my head with oil, but she has anointed my feet with ointment. Therefore I tell you, her sins, which are many, are forgiven, for she loved much; but he who is forgiven little, loves little." And he said to her, "Your sins are forgiven." Then those who were at table with him began to say among themselves, "Who is this, who even forgives sins?" And he said to the woman, "Your faith has saved you; go in peace."

*Before Jesus enters Jerusalem, Matthew, Mark, and John report another anointing of Jesus by a woman. In John's Gospel, the woman doing this anointing is identified as Mary, the sister of Martha and Lazarus. From the time of St. Gregory the Great, this Mary was understood to be Mary Magdalene.*

### John 12:1-8

Six days before the Passover, Jesus came to Bethany, where Lazarus was, whom Jesus had raised from the dead. There they made him a supper; Martha served, and Lazarus was one of those at table with him. Mary took a pound of costly ointment of pure nard and anointed the feet of Jesus and wiped his feet with her hair; and the house was filled with the fragrance of the ointment. But Judas Iscariot, one of his disciples (he who was to betray him), said, "Why was this ointment not sold for three hundred denarii and given to the poor?" This he said, not that he cared for the poor but because he was a thief, and as he had the money box he used to take what was put into it. Jesus said, "Let her alone, let her keep it for the day of my burial. The poor you always have with you, but you do not always have me."

*Finally, this passage from Luke was crucial in interpretations of Mary Magdalene through the Middle Ages. The "Mary," sister of Martha, was understood to be Mary Magdalene, and her contemplative stance in the presence of Jesus became an essential element of her biography, and an inspiration to aspiring contemplatives throughout the Middle Ages.*

## Luke 10:38-42

Now as they went on their way, he entered a village; and a woman named Martha received him into her house. And she had a sister called Mary, who sat at the Lord's feet and listened to his teaching. But Martha was distracted with much serving; and she went to him and said, "Lord, do you not care that my sister has left me to serve alone? Tell her then to help me." But the Lord answered her, "Martha, Martha, you are anxious and troubled about many things; one thing is needful. Mary has chosen the good portion, which shall not be taken away from her."

# Appendix B
# 'GOSPEL OF MARY'

*The* Gospel of Mary *was discovered in 1896, as part of a codex purchased in Egypt. The fragment dates from the fourth century, and the date of composition could have been anywhere between the mid-second century and the fourth century. Most scholars place it midway, in the third century. It contains Gnostic themes, but at least one scholar has argued that it is more expressive of Stoicism than Gnosticism. Only a very few scholars believe that it reveals anything about early Christianity. The title in the codex is simply the* Gospel of Mary, *not the* Gospel of Mary Magdalene, *as some modern editions have it. It is reproduced here in order to demystify its contents, and to help the reader see the great distance, not only in time, but also in content and tone, between these Gnostic writings and the canonical Gospels. (*Source: www.gnosis.org/library/marygosp.htm; the text is reprinted as it appears on the website.)

## Chapter 4

*(Pages 1 to 6 of the manuscript, containing chapters 1–3, are lost. The extant text starts on page 7 . . .)*

. . . Will matter then be destroyed or not?

22) The Savior said, All nature, all formations, all creatures exist in and with one another, and they will be resolved again into their own roots.

23) For the nature of matter is resolved into the roots of its own nature alone.

24) He who has ears to hear, let him hear.

25) Peter said to him, Since you have explained everything to us, tell us this also: What is the sin of the world?

26) The Savior said There is no sin, but it is you who make sin when you do the things that are like the nature of adultery, which is called sin.

27) That is why the Good came into your midst, to the essence of every nature in order to restore it to its root.

28) Then He continued and said, That is why you become sick and die, for you are deprived of the one who can heal you.

29) He who has a mind to understand, let him understand.

30) Matter gave birth to a passion that has no equal, which proceeded from something contrary to nature. Then there arises a disturbance in its whole body.

31) That is why I said to you, Be of good courage, and if you are discouraged be encouraged in the presence of the different forms of nature.

32) He who has ears to hear, let him hear.

33) When the Blessed One had said this, He greeted them all, saying, Peace be with you. Receive my peace unto yourselves.

34) Beware that no one lead you astray saying Lo here or lo there! For the Son of Man is within you.

35) Follow after Him!

36) Those who seek Him will find Him.

37) Go then and preach the gospel of the Kingdom.

38) Do not lay down any rules beyond what I appointed you, and do not give a law like the lawgiver lest you be constrained by it.

39) When He said this He departed.

## Chapter 5

1) But they were grieved. They wept greatly, saying, How shall we go to the Gentiles and preach the gospel of the Kingdom of the Son of Man? If they did not spare Him, how will they spare us?

2) Then Mary stood up, greeted them all, and said to her brethren, Do not weep and do not grieve nor be irresolute, for His grace will be entirely with you and will protect you.

3) But rather, let us praise His greatness, for He has prepared us and made us into Men.

4) When Mary said this, she turned their hearts to the Good, and they began to discuss the words of the Savior.

5) Peter said to Mary, Sister we know that the Savior loved you more than the rest of woman.

6) Tell us the words of the Savior which you remember which you know, but we do not, nor have we heard them.

7) Mary answered and said, What is hidden from you I will proclaim to you.

8) And she began to speak to them these words: I, she said, I saw the Lord in a vision and I said to Him, Lord I saw you today in a vision. He answered and said to me,

9) Blessed are you that you did not waver at the sight of Me. For where the mind is there is the treasure.

10) I said to Him, Lord, how does he who sees the vision see it, through the soul or through the spirit?

11) The Savior answered and said, He does not see through the soul nor through the spirit, but the mind that is between the two that is what sees the vision and it is [. . .]

*(pages 11-14 are missing from the manuscript)*

## Chapter 8

. . . it.

10) And desire said, I did not see you descending, but now I see you ascending. Why do you lie since you belong to me?

11) The soul answered and said, I saw you. You did not see me nor recognize me. I served you as a garment and you did not know me.

12) When it said this, it (the soul) went away rejoicing greatly.

13) Again it came to the third power, which is called ignorance.

14) The power questioned the soul, saying, Where are you going? In wickedness are you bound. But you are bound; do not judge!

15) And the soul said, Why do you judge me, although I have not judged?

16) I was bound, though I have not bound.

17) I was not recognized. But I have recognized that the All is being dissolved, both the earthly things and the heavenly.

18) When the soul had overcome the third power, it went upwards and saw the fourth power, which took seven forms.

19) The first form is darkness, the second desire, the third ignorance, the fourth is the excitement of death, the fifth is the kingdom of the flesh, the sixth is the foolish wisdom of flesh, the seventh is the wrathful wisdom. These are the seven powers of wrath.

20) They asked the soul, Whence do you come slayer of men, or where are you going, conqueror of space?

21) The soul answered and said, What binds me has been slain, and what turns me about has been overcome,

22) and my desire has been ended, and ignorance has died.

23) In a aeon I was released from a world, and in a Type from a type, and from the fetter of oblivion which is transient.

24) From this time on will I attain to the rest of the time, of the season, of the aeon, in silence.

## Chapter 9

1) When Mary had said this, she fell silent, since it was to this point that the Savior had spoken with her.

2) But Andrew answered and said to the brethren, Say what you wish to say about what she has said. I at least do not believe that the Savior said this. For certainly these teachings are strange ideas.

3) Peter answered and spoke concerning these same things.

4) He questioned them about the Savior: Did He really speak privately with a woman and not openly to us? Are we to turn about and all listen to her? Did He prefer her to us?

5) Then Mary wept and said to Peter, My brother Peter, what do you think? Do you think that I have thought this up myself in my heart, or that I am lying about the Savior?

6) Levi answered and said to Peter, Peter you have always been hot tempered.

7) Now I see you contending against the woman like the adversaries.

8) But if the Savior made her worthy, who are you indeed to reject her? Surely the Savior knows her very well.

9) That is why He loved her more than us. Rather let us be ashamed and put on the perfect Man, and separate as He commanded us and preach the gospel, not laying down any other rule or other law beyond what the Savior said.

10) And when they heard this they began to go forth to proclaim and to preach.

# ABOUT THE AUTHOR

**Amy Welborn** is the author of many books, including *Here. Now. A Catholic Guide to the Good Life* and *de-coding Da Vinci: The Facts Behind the Fiction of 'The Da Vinci Code'* (Our Sunday Visitor). She holds a master of arts in Church history from Vanderbilt University.

# Get
## the Facts
## Behind the Fiction
## of The Da Vinci Code

de-coding Da Vinci, The facts behind the fiction of *The Da Vinci Code*, a book by Our Sunday Visitor columnist Amy Welborn, addresses the misrepresentation of history, religion, and art in **The Da Vinci Code**. *Did Leonardo actually build these "codes" into his paintings? Is the Holy Grail really, as he says, Mary Magdalene's womb and now her bones, and not the Last Supper cup? Was Jesus human or divine or both? Was He married to Mary Magdalene? Do secret writings not in the Bible really contain truths about Jesus, Mary Magdalene, and the "sacred feminine"?*

Complete with discussion questions in every chapter, this is the perfect book to accurately answer your questions as well as inspire further faithful discussion and conversation among your peers. Use it either as a personal resource to expand your knowledge of the issues raised by **The Da Vinci Code**, to lead a discussion for your book club or your parish faith community, or to discuss with friends who've read the book and have questions that need to be answered.

**Understand the facts behind the fiction.**
**Order your copy of de-coding Da Vinci today!**

# 1-800-348-2440 x3

**de-coding Da Vinci:**
**The facts behind the fiction of** *The Da Vinci Code*
by Amy Welborn, 1-59276-101-1 (ID# T153)

**Our Sunday Visitor**

200 NOLL PLAZA • HUNTINGTON, IN • 46750

A63BBBBP